WHERE
 # ICARUS
FALLS

at
n."
'. Marinetti

WHERE

ICARUS
FALLS

EDITED BY
MARILYN CHANDLER MCENTYRE

SANTA BARBARA REVIEW PUBLICATIONS
SANTA BARBARA, CALIFORNIA
1998

Published by:
Santa Barbara Review Publications
P.O. Box 808
Summerland, California 93067

Printed in the United States

First Edition 1998

ISBN   0-9655497-3-9

Cover Design: "Where Icarus Falls"
Copyright © 1998 Patricia S. Leddy

INTRODUCTION

—by Marilyn Chandler McEntyre

One of poetry's many purposes is to help us remember elemental things. Think here of remembering as the opposite of dismembering: experiences we may once have taken in whole—as children, say, before the age of analysis, reason, and file cabinets—become disintegrated in the fragmenting procedures, schedules, protocols and conventions of everyday life. Moving from one thing to another, it is easy to miss the wholeness of what one writer called "the personal life deeply lived."

Poets, like ecologists, are finding new ways to utter the call to remembrance that dates back to the Psalms and beyond: remember that you are dust, a mortal creature sharing the earth with others. Remember the voice that speaks in the wind. Remember the refiner's fire. Remember, as Lao Tse taught, that the way of the wise one is the way of water. As we become more and more detached from whole process, from the cycle of seasons, planting and harvest, building and making by hand, we need these reminders more urgently: that we are made from this earth; that, as Donne put it, no man is an island, and as Whitman put it, "every atom belonging to me as good belongs to you," and as Eliot put it, "the river is within us; the sea is all around us."

To invite you to meditate on elemental things, the poems in this collection are grouped under four headings that represent the first "periodic table of elements"—Earth, Air, Water, and Fire. The ancients believed that all things were made of these, and the larger truth of that belief lies in meditation on the subtleties and complexities of each, both in their physical properties and in their symbolic richness.

The "Earth" section begins with poems that direct our gaze to the earth itself, to the flora and fauna of the natural world, the changing topography of land that is turned and gutted and depleted and, as Hopkins put it, "bleared and smeared" by human enterprise. Other poems in this section celebrate the physical life of the body—birth and growth within and away from womb and family, the scars the body bears that tell its story, the ways the body replicates and shares in the primal energies of the universe and in its entropic dwindling toward death. Still others reflect on ways individuals enter into communion with the earth, in gardens, in shaping pots out of clay, in the arts that represent and transform what we touch and see in order that we may know it differently. Several poems lead us to reflect on animals, not as fellow creatures only, but also as objects of our predation and symbols of our confused dominion over life forms we neither know nor own. Finally there are poems about place—cities, wild and open spaces, and roads—that invite us to ponder the ways we range over and inhabit the earth—how we internalize outer landscapes and project inner ones.

Some who study and work with dreams say that flying dreams are empowering. They come as omens of success, signs of hope, reminders from the unconscious that we are more free and powerful than we know. The wish to fly, of course, takes us back to the story of Icarus and his failure, and so flying may also be an idea and image that evokes wistfulness: we can make supersonic jets now, and venture up for an afternoon in colorful balloons or on hang-gliders, but still we can't quite stretch out our own wings and fly. So air and sky remain for us an element as close as our own breath and as remote and ungraspable as heaven or infinity.

The poems in the "Air" section begin with ambiguous images of humans flying (like Antaeus who reflects, "I don't much like it here . . .") that recall those mythic wishes, continuing with several that feature beings who do inhabit the air. We groundlings can travel the skies only with our senses, squinting into the vast light, feeling the movements of the wind and watching it make still things dance. When we dance we suddenly recognize space as a medium, not neutral, but charged with potential syntax and meaning. Several poems in this section focus our attention on sight and light, wind and subtle vibrations that make the air visible, tangible, and pregnant with possibility. The cold of the seasons, the changing qualities of sunlight and shadow, the smells the air carries that sometimes provide our deepest sense of place, all figure in succeeding poems where again and again the wind sweeps through like a leitmotif, gathering resonance, recalling Odysseus' storms, Lear on the Heath, Ecclesiastes' words on the brevity of flesh like grass ("the wind passes over it and it is gone") or the promise of the Spirit that "bloweth where it listeth." The last poems point to sky and stars, the great spaces so filled with the projections of human imagination and testimony to human finitude, where movements of heavenly bodies somehow seem to mirror the movements of the heart for those who have brooded, like Van Gogh, on "starry, starry nights." "Riverrun" is the word Joyce chose to begin and end *Finnegan's Wake*, the most complex and comprehensive novel in English. Rivers run through the long landscape of literature from the Tigris to the Styx to the Thames to the Mississippi. Veins and arteries of the earth, they are still, archetypally and literally, a life source. So the "Water" section begins with river poems, or poems in which the river is a point of departure, leading long and wide into reflection on our ambiguous and amphibious lives— or where it is invoked in its dark and mysterious mutability as "the wide river of what can't be said." These are followed by poems that take us to the shores of oceans where the horizon widens and waves evoke thoughts of power and transiency and children play, unconcerned, in the presence of immensity. From there, several poems turn to ponds and pools where gazers still stand like Narcissus or Thoreau or Annie Dillard at Tinker Creek, pondering the depths and their own purposes. Two poems focus on the boat, also a resonant image whose history from Ark to Pequod to the runaways' raft represents a delicate balance between adventure and safety. A final poem looks at the remnants of ocean life in a dry California canyon, taking the measure of our lives in "Twelve-thousand-year-old shells."

"Fire" is the shortest section, not by design, but perhaps because it is the most elusive of the elements of life. The fire of the sun provides a starting point in "Lumen" where the physics of light push the old metaphor to its extremity. "Transport" continues with a painful focus on the desert sun that seems to absorb what it illuminates. Then fires, destructive, purgatorial, transforming, take us backward through time and inward in poems where fire is the central figure for spiritual life and death.

Each section ends with three haiku—poems so little they can be read rightly only by consenting to a moment of complete stillness. Like the ding of the triangle or the pluck of a string that sounds the last note in the silence when the orchestra stops, these small utterances leave their single notes like after-images, reminding us, perhaps as Eliot did, how "words, after speech, reach / Into the silence."

The poems in this collection, most previously unpublished, though the poets have published widely elsewhere, speak in very different voices, informing one another in unexpected ways. They offer a wide array of experiments in form and so provide a broad sampler of contemporary craftsmanship. And they offer a rich mine of impressions and reminders and perhaps, here and there, a line or angle of vision that succeeds in meeting Pound's demanding requirement of poetry to "make it new."

CONTENTS

viii

EARTH 1

AIR 55

WATER 89

FIRE 117

CONTRIBUTORS 141

EARTH

Hall Canyon / How the Earth Loves Back
(for two voices)

2

banks of flowers, color falls, jolts of blade and leaf
twists, bends, folds whirl the eye
          "here and here and here and over here"
bands of shadow curve the hills,
its soft motions roll songwards
          "let the heart sway and eye follow"
the breather open mouthed
kiss slow respiring on air
          "give warmth to the blossom's deep bow"
the wet stalk cud-sweet
sail-filling sound of petals blown back, so slight,
fragrance of sour pollen
          "straddle my love pouring and purring"
every recess shown.

—Robert Chianese

Rainbow Canyon

Lupine going to seed beside me,
water twisting over granite bench
at my back. More sun,
all sky, still the same Sierra day
John Muir traversed on restless feet,
pondering his angry father,
Disciple of Christ, who bent
his force to sacrifice his oldest son.

The wounds bled here, stigmata
trailing across the slabs and meadows.
Nature drank what she could,
but still, nothing stanched the flow.
Forsaken in the name of God,
where could he turn? Here, at last,
a mother's heart, purple drops
of streamside lupine.

—Paul Willis

Spring, 1997

The world against the wild man is
a world against the wilderness.

The wilderness unabated in us
buys a ticket to lost paradise

where the circus is outroaring
the rooting for the rotting clown

inside the hidden king
under his flattened crown.

—Edwin Honig

Tree

4

I had a tree cut down
a big eucalyptus by the driveway
a messy thing
sharp tacks for berry caps
but it stood a multi-trunk tufted plume
silver graygreen
bark like soaked and softened cardboard.

I had it topped at thirty feet at first:
it brushed the roof, a hazard.
I had it chopped again:
the trimmed ends sent out shoots
of great looping branches
swaying, then leaning out of balance.
It became a scruffy ungainly thing:
each saw cut a spray of shoots
weak, pale green.
It had to come down.

The trimmer shaved and pruned
and pieced it to the ground log by log.
Chunks thudded the yard, the house shook.
And then its double trunk was rotten
a wet chocolaty core
sure to cause big trouble.

Its absence throws light on darkened spots of ground
deep behind the house,
bares some yard that hasn't seen the sky for years.

I stand in fresh rays,
squinty,
mark the space and shape it's left.
Surely that job had to be done.

—Robert Chianese

Poem that Came Out of the Storm

I want to tell you a story
but am anxious you won't listen
nervous the words will pile in the air
like a clutter of ants piling on a spill of honey

5

I want to take you with me through the gate into the wet field
where the rain falls like a cinema screen
and make you believe
whatever I say is true

it is
The wind has never told a lie
The trees have always been true to themselves
the bay laurel bends, the redwood stands

If you cry, if you sit down on the ground and cry
and then you know the shape of your ribs
how they hold hurt and relief, how they release
then you are the wiser for it,
then you have likeness to trees
leaning off the steep slope in the open

then you are a little like moss,
then you are green and a bed
and can make life with what is fallen

and if you are like the gravel where you sit
so much the better, wisdom
never came soft or easy
And the gravel is on the path
and the gravel is in the soggy field

Sometimes you will wake with the gravel in your throat
or stumble through the light with gravel in your eyes
or, listening to the wind be true through the trees, your ears
will be full of gravel
And you may think, What a stony way!
And you may wonder, Where is the peace of ponds and lily pads?
May finally ask, When will the water wash this rubble down?

Well, then we will come into the field of rain that falls
and make ready to believe,
and lay in with the bees for spring

—Mandy Richmond Dowd

Orange

for my mother

1.
Scrape a pumpkin clean,
cut a smile on the doorstep—
seeds saved in a silver pan.

2.
A ship of mashed yams
on my Thanksgiving plate—
eat hot orange, thick orange,
mouthfuls of orange.

3.
Boots, belt, the shouting lips
of Santa; color him orange,
blood orange—a huge dripping beard.

4.
It was all I could do.

5.
The last thing I remember
is your face in front of the kitchen window,
your orange curls, arched, flared in the sun.

6.
I jumped, ripping oranges,
from the tree behind the house
when you left. I tore in
from their navels, and ate their dry white roots.

—Allison Benis

Oranges

Her breath stills the green frame as he meant
it to. Her ripening body lowers in a white dress
stippled with the painter's palette knife.
Orange starts, enough of them to count,

spring like musical notes from the deep field.
She would like to lie down but has been made
to stand composed against the agitation of his eye.
His goatee is autumn gone to seed.

His jacket, ripped at the pocket, falls
from his bent bones like a shroud.
The wrinkled neck is noosed beneath
the hollow eyes. His palette burns.

The fields beyond the place are ripe with greens
and grapes, nurtured things for a winter's feeding.
She and he who has the paints and eye
to stop her find themselves in flowers.

They practice how it's done, those two, what
it takes to score the heart with oranges.

—Martin Galvin

For Fertility

8

One of them is blackberries,
now raisined on the bush.
One is yellow apples
in the grass of empty trees.
One is red stars from the sweet-gum,
wax-coated in the window.
And one is lacy cabbages,
pink as candy in the center,
unfolding, unfolding all winter.

—Ila R. Asplund

New Father
—*for Stephen Sandy*

When you named your son
in the poem and read in public
how he woke always
on your nights of love,
I trusted the man
who had striven through
since I had heard and read
you last.
And if you love your own words much
it has only worked them richer
till the glitter of their fruit
ingresses to purify the gift.
And I see how art
fulfills itself in giving
as a burst of seed
into convulsing vessel
makes each perfect child.

—Josephine Carson

The Son

Their lightness became a thatch of weeds
dispersed behind the backyard fence, formless,
but as new as forgetting your own death.
That day, you simply pushed the wheelbarrow

of soil through the slapboard gate, as if
in a snub, worn hearse. They loved you deeply
once, but they own nothing but grass and sky
in the quiet glade out back. Before long,

you have left other homes behind, so as
to avoid lovelessness, the hush of habit,
And while those doors lock shut, that one gate
remains open. There are your parents,

still waving up at you, happy as mulch.
You get up in the morning and they wave
and wave. On the weekends, you fix coffee
and sit, charming them from the breakfast nook.

Such a nice man. You were never their son.

—Kevin Clark

THE VIEW FROM PURDAH

Husband and Son Arriving

One is my child and
one my chosen child.
One is all himself; one
half his.
One is half the other and
half me, himself
altogether held against
time.
That one owns me.
One summons in secret
her whose he always
will be, as that small one
will be mine and me,
as I, his last whispered
word, will be all his.

Mother of Sons

Your house shakes and
loses shape
stuffed with the truck of their lives.
Their punishing footfalls
mutilate some space you waxed
last week.
But when that tree fell in the yard
they were both off camping.

Alone you hunt those rooms
for the vagrant selves
they keep. You turn the music
high and howl till you can sleep.
You curl back like a snake.

When will you make that leap
across for the self caught
in this past?
Do you already guess
you'll become the last word
in an old son's mouth
and his only rest?

New Women

They graze
not safely
in fields of doubt
and wonder,
lately sundered and
unhoused of past
whose gazes lift at evening
to no last hunter
home wounded
or with gift of kill, but
to some still unnamed prey
that they themselves
just were
and now, without knife
or skill but only hunger,
must run to ground
and sacrifice.

—Josephine Carson

For Chul Ung's Face at Night

12

I never did care for the palm of the hand.
It's sweaty or cold, a cup
of grime where my love line and death
line and life line connect—
I'll not touch it to your face.

I'd rather the back of the hand
where I'm soft with velvet
hair in each bamboo notch
between knuckles. Mine are marked
with three little stars, flickering
schoolyard pavement: gravel
that might still be there.

I prefer just the tip
of each finger, wish I could peel
back the nail and leave only the
white crescent moons. When I touched
your face, they'd at least be good
cold, like a live autumn night
that tastes of leaves, of a day
much colder—the fleshy pads
clean, playing arabesques,
and you would listen.

—Ila R. Asplund

Somnambulist

She's there, an increasingly fragile figure in the garden
The cat she calls hers strops itself about her ankles
The tails of a faded plaid shirt flap slightly as she moves
Sensibly-shod, her narrow feet pick a path around the gopher mounds

The cat she calls hers strops itself about her ankles
A few of the birds she feeds are perched on sagging fence posts
Sensibly shod, her narrow feet pick a path around the gopher mounds
From the slopes above, the bells on Roxor's goats ring random melodies

A few of the birds she feeds are perched on sagging fence posts
She leans on her spade handle, mops her brow with a bandanna
From the slopes above, the bells on Roxor's goats ring random melodies
Beyond the trees, a vulture wheels in silent circles, but she will not see it

She leans on her spade handle, mops her brow with a bandanna
Her fingers, rough-pricked from years of quilting, catch in the soft, sodden cloth
Beyond the trees, a vulture wheels in silent circles, but she will not see it
The air is dense with insects. One lands on her neck, beneath the collar

Her fingers, rough-pricked from years of quilting, catch in the soft, sodden cloth
She bends, stiffly, disentangles a bean tendril from its neighbor, straightens
The air is dense with insects. One lands on her neck, beneath the collar
She turns and eyes the cat, which stalks a vivid butterfly nearby

She bends, stiffly, disentangles a bean tendril from its neighbor, straightens
The mincing step she takes next crushes a large worm. She would be sorry, if she noticed
She turns and eyes the cat, which stalks a vivid butterfly nearby
From the bright white house behind her come sounds of a viola, playing Haydn

The mincing step she takes next crushes a large worm. She would be sorry, if she noticed
Her shoulders stiffen. Gophers have annexed another bell pepper
From the bright white house behind her come sounds of a viola, playing Haydn
She fumbles an ancient cigarette case free from her shorts-pocket

(cont.)

14

Her shoulders stiffen. Gophers have annexed another bell pepper
In revenge, she lobs a weed at a red-winged blackbird, and misses
She fumbles an ancient cigarette case free from her shorts-pocket
Two violins join in playing the Haydn, both off-pitch and unpunctual

In revenge, she lobs a weed at a red-winged blackbird, and misses
During a momentary silence, a sudden jay shrieks Quit-quit-quit-quit
Two violins join in playing the Haydn, both off-pitch and unpunctual
The butterfly falls victim to the cat; two half-wing fragments offer testimony

During a momentary silence, a sudden jay shrieks Quit-quit-quit-quit
The tails of a faded plaid shirt flap slightly as she moves
The butterfly falls victim to the cat; two half-wing fragments offer testimony
She's there, an increasingly fragile figure in the garden

—Annie Stenzel

Aubade

bed covers still
       warm
after the morning trip to the
       bathroom
the body disperses heat so
       quick
hot wires in an open toaster

earth still
       warm
after our short trip under the
       sun
mother soil keeps us cradles us
from absolute
       zero

the corpse in cool
       suspension
long gestation under ground
       then
bed pillow the dreamless sleeper
       collapse
bits and pieces rejoin the fathers'
shimmering motions 'round the firey
       stars

until the death of
       heat
the end of all
       urges
including the glorious morning
       pee

—Robert Chianese

Utterance

16

Centering always comes first
     after wedging the clay, that is,
     and thumping it down on the wheelhead
     and sponging it slippery slimy wet
Hands close over the leftward spinning earthen mound
elbows tuck in tightly
     and from the set of the jaw
     to the focused purpose
     of rigid wrists and fingers
wordless and breathless squeezing
eases the lump into roundness

Never before
in twelve years hunched over the potter's wheel
has the clay found
true center
through these hands

Usually
even after the effort
a wobble remains
a waver at the base
     or halfway up
     barely noticeable
     and inconsequential
and so I continue on

This time, though,
through some accident, perhaps,
of unaccustomed energy or concentration
the clay
     though spinning
appears motionless
     rock solid
     as still and full as the moment before speech
     or the pregnant
     empty page

The silence of the unformed mass
draws me in and holds me
I surrender

EARTH

                suspended and solitary
Reluctant to press on
                to press a hole in the center
                dislodging it from center
from the whole and pure premise of this moment

For the bowl will be flawed
The line will lack grace, no doubt,
                betraying its potential
                off-balance
                it will sit too heavy in the hand

Yet clay demands form
The primal elements
                earth and water
                air and fire
transmuted through the potter's craft
                combine
enclosing space in stonefired permanence
the pot declares itself

And the bowl will hold barley soup
                or strawberries
                or air
It will pass from my hands to yours
And there is life
                and chance
                in the warped, imperfect curve of the lip
and commitment in the offering

And so
with fingers resting lightly
on the smoothly spinning surface
I linger
                in this mute and formless center
                briefly
                longingly
And tugging
and aching
press thumbs downward
to open the pot

—Jane Fremon

Erasion

18

My mother hated her own paintings
She copied most of them from snapshots
And if the image didn't measure up
She'd whitewash over it
Our attic, a graveyard of discards
Was filled with these white expanses
Cobwebbed castoffs aborted by the artist in mid-bloom
They'd lie in wait until she revisited their barren spaces
She painted a portrait of me
From a stilted studio photo
She worked feverishly while I watched
But the subject was not allowed to touch the brushes
As she dipped and swept, the painting neared completion
I wondered then if she'd ever whitewash me
When I dropped her Mexican clay owl I feared it
When she caught me smoking one of her cigarettes, I fretted
I don't recall what set her off
As she ran the unforgiving sable bristles
Through her Scotch glass and into the white paint
Erasing her latest mistake in a fraction of the time it took to
create
Because it was never quite pretty enough, thin enough. . . never quite
enough
I stood trembling in a white-hot darkness
How long until she started over on me?
To hear her tell it, she never laid a brush on me
Revisionist! She altered my landscape with the weight of a looming
threat
I lay petrified in that kiln of an attic
Alongside the dusty antiquities
Until I found the courage
To escape its narrow confines
When I finally dared to caress the treasured brushes
And tax the strength of their wooden handles with my own hands
I knew I'd never paint backwards across a canvas that is me
I glance back with fondness at my breadcrumbed trail
It enables me to stand in the face of the blinding sun
Reversing the direction of my yet-unpainted path

—Cindy LaFavre Yorks

Familiar

I am going to take this up
with the darkness, the fact

that I might die now
sooner, sooner than old

dusk, cusp of evening like a cup
the remains of the day pour in

darkness, a gentle fold of peace
I wait in your wing

for what—what are facts
but little nubs to prove,

disprove, hard as nails
sunken into soft

ply of pine, sunk
with ease into dirt, loam

& mystery: listen into
the granular sound of earth

turning soil on soil she rolls
lumbrous around the sun

but rolls
                    rolls on

the dark, a soft glove
on her face turned away

turning the way we came

—Mandy Richmond Dowd

Uncle

The bud stands for all things.
                    —Galway Kinnell

We are named
at our deaths
by the small wishes
that attend us,
the hungry blue buds
of monks hood
of larkspur.

You mouthed for
a hamburger
with onions and relish,
circled soup-du-jour
on the hospital menu,
left your wife
wishing she'd had
a bit of chocolate
the rest of her life.

—Arthur Nahill

POETS
Born Crossed
   re: Anne Sexton

In late pictures
she looked as if born crossed,
her face become scissors
crossed at the nose,
cut deep at the mouth's corners,
foxed at the fork between eyes
right and left.
It seemed two women battled there
and no wars won or lost
but some right lost at birth,
a first ore bled out at christening,
twin and mother both washed out,
and the final scar a closure
in the room of bright roses.

Life in the Trees

I like to be with the old man
poets now.
They have learned how to stay
home with smart old humorous wives.
They sit, the old poets,
and watch the myriad small forms
of life out in the trees where
poetry, exhausted, flew to roost,
to hide its head through
the long sterile season.
Like nestlings among leaves,
old poets wait, they hum
phrases idly torn.
They will perform if coaxed
the small chores of home
in long gestures unencumbered
by memory as though nothing
had ever been done before
                              or said.

—Josephine Carson

Upon Seeing Willa Cather's Grave at Jaffrey Center

It's worth a visit
but the stone is wordy.
They had to speak
        who buried her
and wouldn't let her name suffice
nor let her bones
        wise enough when living
probe the long passage
back to silence.
The tongue submits in gratitude,
but how could they know?
Willa never would condone
more than the slow effacement
of her name
        upon that stone.

—Josephine Carson

Hymn to Her

The load you take
is dense, backbreaking
and mistaken.

It may be otherwise
as when, in full light
wholly undertaken,

the load grows slim
and, to one
that takes it, bracing—

owed to none
but to the life
that lifts awakened.

—Edwin Honig

2

2

FAMILY PLOT
Pieta

23

The small world has a picture
of our pieta, Mother—
you down from your cross at last—
but it fails to show how after
the shutter's click you break
and like a great tree in a flood crack
through my knees, your flesh bone blood
rush into time's quick
tracking the drift of it you go.
And that's all I know
of giving birth.
My cramped sight shifts its lens,
strains out to where you end
as sky. My head's room with a wall
knocked out gapes and
my arms lift air. Just there
I keep my marble watch.

Omen

Thirty years before you fired
the gun at your head,
you and I squatted in the grass
and cried warning
as the girl sauntered across
to the coop after the chicken
her long black patient arm
swinging, the bright flash
of the cleaver's blade—
in her arm how it weighed down!
By all this she would teach us
how to live in the world
you would later blow away.
And then the swift catch,
slam of the chicken gone mute
onto the stump

(cont.)

and the cleaver's single crack.
She said—"Don't cry. This chicken
                              don't need no head. Looky there!"
where the spastic flying feathery headless
thing careened the yard.
And we children sickened,
stared at the stopped eye and knew
that tonight this host would be offered us
and we would eat.

Desperate Service

That poor neighbor
deluded himself that he wanted me.
He tried to fix my car.
Stumbling, he carried the big
blue packages of our laundry
and rolled in the oxygen tank.
All summer he plotted
this desperate service
while the very day of her death
formed itself in the careless city
and in my spare stalled furious life
that would be laid open
right next door to him.

Family Plot

He must have thought through
the correct timing of it
like a self-winding spring,
must have waited for her to come
as witness,
perfecting that one move—his last—
from the pocket where he gripped
the gun to his temple and
the trigger-finger's order—
                one fast slam in the barrel.
He must have dared the very image
of his blown skull and craved all
those forty years avenged,
loathing his sloth in the face of
this act,
and cared not to balance against
such precision just how
her life would follow—
                hearing her then in the other room
                clearing her throat,
                a scrape of hangers along the pole—
                Oh, when would she come?
Or did he see us all blown away
with him, to be resurrected later
as one body?
It's true—we keep his vision now,
trapped here in the shot's long
echo, wrapped in his dream—
this last unbreakable bond.

—Josephine Carson

L'Espoir du Desespoir
—*To Monsieur Jean Passerat ("Inventor" of the Villanelle)*

26

I recommend you undertake despair.
Challenge yourself. Admit you cannot fix
the part of hope that lies in disrepair.

Declare how "fair is foul and foul is fair."
Take this *bon mot* to heart, and when it sticks,
I recommend you undertake despair.

"*Facile, j'espère,*" you say. "*Elementaire!*"
To this "*espoir*" I urge you to affix
the parted "*des-*" that lies in dis-repair.

In time you'll find you really couldn't care
that Frenchy maledictions come to nix.
I recommend you. Undertake despair:

The undertaker looks so debonair
each night he lies beneath the crucifix
imparting hope that lies in Dis. Repair

takes place below, where Proserpine must bear
her paradox, where Thanatos plays tricks,
ends what it takes to undertake despair:
the part of hope that lies. In Dis, repair!

—Stephen Massimilla

Trophies

Boys kill small animals for sport:
first dawning of self, first fears of death and
ants twist in the magnifier's ray.

We bee-bee-ed dragonflies,
our sling shots cut from plywood,
        and Whammo bands,
leather pouches from old belts—
weapons birds trembled to think of.
        Zen-like, we
ripped bugs from the pond's hot breath.
They sewed your eyes shut,
        deserved it,
flashing, falling, neon blues and greens.

We steel-balled turtles,
bagged their sunny stupor,
        elegant sliders,
the red cheek-gash our aiming spot,
fitted shells, mosaics, thunked apart.

We let toads and frogs and all birds go,
and no occasional cat,
        I promise,
though we stung the pink udders of MacGalliard's cows
and dared our cartoon dreams:
farmer racing up the hill,
straps flying,
blasting fannies.

I shot-put a heavy stone:
a blue jay pecked the ground,
        sad luck
for that squirming miracle.

(cont.)

28

Rats roamed the sludge piles at the sewage plant.
      Now with 22's,
our bolts front-pocketed,
we strolled the suburb to its edge,
      dangerous, nonchalant.
           (Who allowed this?
           Call the police.)
They clutched their wounds, flipped, and died.

Our Baja boatmen
made us go after the marlin all in a row.
"Merlino! Merlino!" and I hooked up,
fought hard,
exploded a spool,
handheld the line while we spliced another reel,
      fish coiling,
the weary prince of those blue blue waters.
They bashed its head:
in an hour in the open punta,
      a brown dull log of meat.
The pobros cheered us on the beach
slicing steaks, running red, "like pork,"
singing the fish's strength and size,
      our oldest song,
luck and prowess.
They knew and loved the fish we fed them.

      Early on
animals roamed limestone walls,
      totems, clan-signs,
caverns of magic sound
where chants bounced and called beasts to death.
      The hunter
takes the spirit with the flesh;
what he takes is fully his.

—Robert Chianese

Hand Game

On a morning-brushed prairie hill
hands stipple in
a boy sitting
still
in light and ink.

Memory opens its grip
on me
sighting along a rifle
watching prairie dogs' witch-black eyes watching back,
penitents kneeling in light-streaked weeds.

I still can hear pencil-thin bullets split fur and bone.

Now on hand-sewn rugs
                           I hug
corners of talk and watch
others watching back.

When Dad died
he held out his arms
lurid-veined,
whitening palms opening for me to see
which hand something was in:

the child's game
I never used to win.

                        —Steve Cook

An Old Dog Decides Where to Die

30

Behind the barn, in the thick veins of sumac
and gaunt shadows of rusted rakes,
he wedges himself, driven
to find a darkness remote, yet familiar.

Plodding toward the pear tree
abandoned on the side of the house,
he sniffs the shallow cradle
of exposed roots. Pears
rot on the ground, yellow shrunken
heads, sticky with bees.

He turns like a rusty hinge,
More comfortable under
the porch, close to the house—
he'll settle in the groove
his body has worn after years
of escaping summer's incessant heat,
where he has already buried his bones.

—Meg Kearney

Western Romance Novels

I.
The Widow Bridewell
at the Double Bar Ranch
sends out anonymous love notes
tucked into tumbleweed.

II.
The Dry Goods on Main
sells buffalo rags
for mechanics
and gun grease for wedlock.

III.
Each tree that you see
has been planted, he said,
water carried in buckets
like tears to a bride.

IV.
The Ladies' Home Sewing Guild
crochets barbed wire
bedjackets for shut-ins
whether they want them or not.

V.
At night by the campfire
the cowboy sings low
all the songs that he knows
to the only kine that will listen.

—Linden F. Ontjes

Tucked Within the Himalayas

Somewhere in a bayul*
lies Khembalung   secret rhododendron jungle
where mind merges with peace.

Believed to have an invisible palace
hunters and herders who wander there
never return.

But Khembalung calls   so I answer
allowing shepherds, bearded and full of stories
to guide me.

Months we journey into uninhabited land
Everest peering down   beautiful, alluring,
cold, and blistery.

An old woman, toothless and wrapped in alpaca colors
tells me of a shrine   "From there look across the valley
see naga**   point the way to Khembalung."

Granite glaciers drip
twists into cobra   head drawn back to strike
as other guardian deities form mist   hide path.

Between ice-peak spirits   around cliff-guardians
I weave down into rock-sheltered valley and walk over the
stream-cushioned meadow.

In morning's light an
invisible palace emerges
among forest pine and thick rhododendron.

Gold mist rises like smoke off trees
water drops gleam blue   diamonds on hanging moss
brown shadows and emerald leaves shape tapestries
line corridors   beckon   bow greeting.

EARTH

Childhood fantasies press forward
primeval jungle feels oddly familiar.

I've been here before.

Thirsty, I kneel at water's edge
drink from my hands   feel Spirit flow
reach the bayul of my soul.

At night, in protected tent
snow-spirit taps   loud and incessant
wind-spirit sings   howls
worry drives away sleep.

But Khembalung's gift reminds
of soul's bayul
and life unfolds here   as if there.

At day break   I return through the clouds.
Like others who wandered here
I do not return
     the same.

*hidden valleys within the Himalayas. Very difficult and dangerous to reach.
**serpent

—Mediha Saliba

Charge

Follow everything where it leads. Strange places.
You wander the will to its edge, peer past the known
            and what? An inkling.
A wide pool of inklings you've swum by night by night,
            walking with wet feet in the day.
                        The willow leans into the lake dipping fronds
                                    at her own reflection
She holds a sky in her unfolded arms, and she is greenness untold
            Breakfast of your young eyes

Keeping faith is a tricky walk of promise and casting off
You turn at the call and weigh
the tone in the walls of your house . . .

            Try this: acting as if
is a wondrous prayer in itself.
Bray like an ass in the stall,
this will beatify even the beast
Cry. Tell the host and guest alike, head
            into the hills, not to hide,
but to rises and valleys tucked after the thought
Bring ceremony home as an ash to the fire
Ear to the window, widow
your wholesome comprehensions
widow the cared-for and the borrowed
widow the shallows hugged ashore
Stand to wind and hear

a hustler harassing the night.
This begins to spell: the test is everything that is and nothing
            less telling
You are but the hand of our meaning, be that
            with your clamp on the hold of ink and wash
Watch the words spill by your foolish heart, in you there is room
            to dance

Be we still then for only the briefest moments
            and these are but a blink of what you think, eh?
Bring us to your brood and blood
Bring us up to the sight of the whole hell
Your wellness warped by
            only unswerved sets of endings

Time will secede,
and what will spill will spill from the open crevices
You go with your axe and splay
Every shard a bit to see by

—Mandy Richmond Dowd

On the Road from Istanbul to Troy
Tuesday, September 15

       To live in a house with
a blue door
and two windows
The land
plowed by a man
with a white horse & cart
       And the waveless sea
holding the red-prowed
boat silent against the
minareted grass shore

       The earth
turns   fresh   moist   and
old
Troy   layered   and
rising
as we watch

       —Jeanne Nichols

On the Road from Antalya to Alana, Sunday, September 27

36

        On the right-hand side of
Emel's five-ton truck a
photograph of his small
son guards the door

        And on the
center panel two
quail, seven rows of blue
tulips, five red-roofed houses, one hump-backed
bridge, one blue stream with six swans in a watery
quadrille, and two sheep safely graze on a
green meadow in a painted town with a
painted purple mountain   while
Emel drives bales of cotton
on the highway between
Antalya to Alan

        After the call
from the tower when
he can tell the difference between a black
thread and a white
he prays

        Now he rests over a glass of chai
at the cafe in front of
the gypsy camp and behind
the diesel station
All the men
drink their chai and
watch the trucks
the trucks of Polat and Akdogan and
Zivorik painted with roses and lilies and
scenes of lakes and forests and mountains
the heavy bright containers of
grey bags of cement and baled
cotton and frantic-eyed mounds
of sheep

        Emel   son of
Noah   keeper of the ark
in the hot wet
Anatolian air
        Ararat waiting
a little way
to the east

—Jeanne Nichols

Tramping

The soles of my shoes've worn thin enough
to feel small pebbles underfoot beneath the vinyl.
Hard stones on these campus roads are most likely
cement ground up and giving forth its rubble,
but the dust of the Island still clings to me like
muscle memory to feet that can find their way
in a dark three thousand miles from home.

Green leather, slope-toed, two-inch heels were
just the ticket most nights there, tramping me
down sandy unlit paths through maple and oak
to the marina bulkhead and the Circuit crawl.

They took me dancing through crowded floors
of summer folk, then back out of doors and around
the Tabernacle's snaking circles. Those had begun
with tents, and I joked that my penchant for high heels
was surely camp. But it was a term lost on
the twenty-two-year-old Econ graduate escorting
me through the fog one night. And though
he was fond of tangents and eager to learn whatever
I might teach him, I was too footloose and free
of fancy to put my pumps beneath his bed.

—Sharon Page

Secondary Road

38

The concrete road was broken
but its tar strips webbed
like veins, the dark life
moving to keep this flat space
linking other spaces, stitched
one hill to another, till,
yes, it coursed itself
beneath the Olds, beneath
the cars of others, even trucks
that growled in second gear
and spilled their fluids
like a rain, gruff-engined
lives what all remorse is
finally: heavy oil and sweat,
the ooze of tar between
one's toes in August, one's
heels burned to keep the dance
across the surface, one eye
cocked for semis lost
within this space where
Interstates die droning
just beyond the hill,
but this, a grey line
on some county map perhaps,
but the white space in the hell
that is cartographer's heaven.

—Robert Parham

Sabbatical

Climbing Shepherd Crest today
in the windless calm of mid-September
I see at last as clearly as I see
Lyell and Half Dome, white and dark
and risen and sunken in the distance,
the truth that I am not in school,
laboring to say things about poetry.

All the perfect days gone by
past office windows,
foothills and blue skies, hardly seen
for explications to be marked—
and then the trauma of handing them back,
the steepening anger in their eyes,
the stormy whispers.

The poems here are the peaks themselves.
I scan them with my soles, my palms,
in the tactile way that students doubt.
I climb, or not, as desire takes me,
and do not demand that anyone follow,
that anyone put words in places
the heart has not already gone.
I am still arriving, the blessedness
of stony silence.

—Paul Willis

Hall Canyon / Two Warnings
            for Peter Alexander

Against living greens and browns
two discs flash
black orange caution:
            "Warning!
            Oil pipes and natural gas.
            Call toll free."
They skewer the hills,
ridge their backs,
a manic cross hatch of lines from the 30's,
hundreds of miles of them,
gullied, shifting,
twelve-inchers swelled to a yard by cement,
unraveling the hills where they pierce them.

The workers, hot, wacked the rattlers,
shooed sheep, drove the big shovel
up and down a roving line
somebody drew and paid for in an office.
At night coyotes sniffed the cold metal treads.

They can't stay,
even if they hold
over the knifeblade creek
or save the hills from houses
creeping up other canyons.
The signs warn themselves:
            "We're going, we're sliding away.
            We'll soon run out.
            You're lost without us."
Drill pipes become fence posts
for a couple hundred years.
The service road withers,
its asphalt already crumbled
by tobacco trees and creosote.
The sleek coyotes will miss its easy path
and the cattle's overflowing trough.
We'll find a cleaner way to tap the sun,
which turned the hills
dry, very dry
too soon this year.
One day we'll walk
the junglegym pipes,
in the obsolete technology playyard.

—Robert Chianese

Municipal Ride

This is it. This is the world I live in.
I am a fragment of its fullest expression.
I ride the bus, pass through the tunnels:
the populace of the city, a random gathering of fragments
of its fullest expression

& you are a piece of it too
In your hand I find
a thread meets a thread
filaments of the states you named:
fear, anger, love, desire, primary
colors blended with the gritty soil of our daily lives

Now brown & bone & beige
the colors coming up in our skin
fishbelly white, the mixing up of the many
Here to work it out

—Mandy Richmond Dowd

Winter Street

He seems an apparition of the snow;
a whitewash of man and after-man—
a piece of business with the world unsettled.
With knotted brow and knitted tie—
he returns.

Ornery flakes swirl about him like bees—
he pays no notice; shows no trace
of wear for the distance he has come.
And with feet so determined toward this destination
his eyes seem unaware of a place in transition:
         a rabble of storefront signs
                in new alphabets; hand painted;
         the butcher, who held on to scraps for the dog,
              is gone;
         the candy store and sarsaparilla,
           pastry shop and charlotte russe—
gone to where sweet dreams go.

We tried to send you off with them,
but you keep finding a way back
in those flimsy shoes so laughable—
on this journey in particular—
yet now I wear them every day too.

Does this satisfy you? Or shall
we meet here next time
                in a steely rain
pounding atop our heads unbowed,
so proud, so crowned with thorns.

—Ron Lawrence

The Leave-Takers

Dick Whittington's cat; Highgate Cemetery in spring rain:
the reckless weeds making a religion of green
around George Eliot's remains
and the bust of Karl Marx—
atheist, communist, bearded British Museum researcher—
cranky, glowering, lording it over the funeral procession
of a dozen black-coated Moslem Yugoslavian refugees
who left a brace of lilacs
beneath the copper beech.

—John Drexel

The Elect

Such geographies, such love.
My map does not show factories
with men working or not working,
men picketing; or women
washing, waiting, watching telly
in tight little terrace houses.
It does not name parties,
tell how votes are counted.
If you were here at this moment
on this train between Huddersfield and Stalybridge
you would reach for my hand,
counseling "on English trains
we needn't keep our love out of sight."
Your eyes would make me a prisoner.
You would ignore this green valley,
the industrial decay, the habitually overcast
Yorkshire sky. "Look," you'd whisper,
disguising your neuroses in a gesture
of shyness, pointing to the little girl
down the carriage: "That's the child
we'll never have together. The child
that could make me legitimate, complete."
You are a gypsy craving a talisman,
a magic ring, a rose. Not in this life,
my love. Not in this life.

—John Drexel

Chicago

At one time even sides of beef
nibbled at stray tufts of weeds.

Then somebody bought an election,
and someone else
invented the 1920s. And
the whole city began reveling
at the Mayor's birthday bash
to some sotted Marimba King's
awkward tune.
                                Once, peppergrass
grew beneath the bloody carcasses.
Grain trucks sprinkled husks of wheat
up and down Water Street. Shafts
of direct sunlight stung
nervous citizens. Real Italian
sopranos lived on every block.

There was a kind of clarity to it all.
A mutt's yelp spiced
the sonic stew. To watch a trapeze
artist in chartreuse tights strolling
down Michigan Avenue at midday was as ordinary
as distilling one's own bathtub gin.

When I came to town,
the web the realtors wove
dissected all counter-narratives. Yoked
to our homes and yards, racked
by niggling guilt, we cowered
in our hives. The drones insisted
that we never see the dawn or stars
or winter fog clinging like warm breath
to the shafts of black glass and grey steel.

 Now, after years of darkness,
jostling for a seat on the Orange Line
amid the smells of garlic, cologne and sweat,
I suddenly realize I can parse
the complex sentence of the faces
all around me, can distinguish
between past and present
and untangle, at last, I and them from we.

—David Starkey

Oklahoma City

often the story takes place in
the car on the way to her mother's house
—some Christian holiday—
bouquet on the back seat or
perhaps a loaf of fresh bread—she's
a wonderful baker and
loves her mother—
right hand draped over
the steering wheel, the
whiteness of her knuckles the
only indication of unspoken awareness—
a bright spot on the upholstery where a
child's car seat is
no longer

 and sometimes the story will
take place when he jogs
in the dry morning the flat streets
of the city past a small
playground more silent than past Saturdays

then again one day the
story may take place in the
abrupt pause in conversation
as you wheel a shopping cart past
clusters of women in
aisles where
clouds of disposable diapers nest near
toilet paper and paper towels

sometimes the story takes place
miles outside the city where
a street dweller digging for bottles to
turn in for five cents each
trips over a bright plastic
Big Wheel,
front wheel melted,
grotesquely orange and yellow in
a sea of decaying suburbia

—Colleen Lindsay

La Selva

Hecha de rejas y hojas,
de amor entre humo.
Un calor de alas rojas
y tráfico hundido.
Hecha de ríos enjaulados
y vientos de petrolio,
de símbolos eternos
y mitologías marcadas.
El correr
de máquinas verdes.
Las fragancias
de piel bajo sombra
y flores sin nombre.
El sudor de ilusiones.
El canto
de instrumentos salvajes
y un corriente de voces.

—Gustavo Alberto Garcia Vaca

El Pueblo de Nuestra Señora Reina de Los Ángeles, California

The desire is to build cities
out of dust, out of brush,
in glass, stone, and flame.
Claims have been used
to fill the vastness
of this unowned land:
but just as wind crossing
the surface of palm leaves,
these names scatter
under the burning sun.

—Gustavo Alberto Garcia Vaca

Little City Inscapes

The pause of urban dark before
daylight's moving violations.
Fog seep and loft, the lure of fires,
of water, of zoos,
of anything roasted.
Horned speech of drifting ships on the black
rocking bay.
Late night walkers tolling love,
its slow spondee.
Foul defoliated sleep of bums; underthrum; snore
of collective gratitude in the fall
of doubters' dark.

        The Mayor's cheap deep concern
        The D.A.'s guarantee
        The Fire Chief's regrets
        The phone operator's luxurious patience
        The dialer's faith
        Industry's apologies
        The agony of ambulances
        The cool of hearses
        The curses of gamblers
        The rambles of panhandlers
        Asian Mafia Murders
        Legal rights and solemn rites
        Cranky crack and crackerjack
        Hard rock and Birkenstocks
        Large Medium and Small
        The policeman's last arrest—Cardiac.

Downtown Deep Six Tone Deaf Thai Dye Dim Sum Te Deum

        Clogged chutes
        Stained glass
        Land Lords
        Crash of markets
        Thud of dropped names at tired tables
        Noble old fairies, young gays

(cont.)

Aiding Aids
Placement tests in certain places
Eternal deliveries
Lapcats and Catscans
Evictions and predilections
Vast majorities
in mixed medias rest.
For break fast - eggs benedict, ex benedict
                    Ex Benedictus
           Pacem in Sodom Urban Absurdum.

The city's only hope in two birds
singing in a window box
its own moonblight sonata.

Small earthquakes, ubiquitous, tolerated
and, like junior partners, cautiously
respected for their potential.

Lucy in her Reboks, formerly of the sky
with diamonds, now jogging four miles a day
out JFK Way to the shore
and back.

Hiding in Pacific Heights—the same old dandy
in the same old Brooks Brothers paternity suit.

The six-year-old son of the Chinese laundry owner
stole two hundred dollars from the laundry cash
register last week, took it to school in his tiny
backpack to pay off two large nine-year-old
girls - one white, one black—who weren't satisfied
anymore with his Dim Sum lunches
and his Gatorade money.

The tiny balding widowed arthritic German
psychiatrist hums *Götterdammerung* and nibbles
mints alone in her opera box at matinee
intermission.

EARTH

With the falling dark, the street ghosts
claim their halls and entryways, winter
whispering them inside like stale winds
whining in lightwells. The huge swaying
bag lady with blackened feet lies smoking
cigarette butts on a spread out sheet of
The Wall Street Journal in our basement
again, where once—its reek still random
there—barreled bootleg wine soaked the sod
floors, seeped into wood table tops.

Sicilian papas drank it, flipped their cards,
were caught Chianti-red-handed and escaped,
leaving their bare-breasted calendar sweeties
abandoned on the wall, accusing, to snake through
tunnels under the Bocci Ball courts beyond
Columbus Ave. to the basement of the doctor
who had always kept them alive and even
delivered them and their slippery sons
into the crooked new land.

Now a small neat brown Szechuan sub-family
biscuit in a wide shallow-crowned hat croons
low in Nolo Bado Naga Kachin—a branch
of the Tibeto-Burmese sub-family
of the Sino-Tibetan family of languages—
to her swaddled biscuit grandchild
in a basket baking on a bench below
the belltowers of St. Peter and St. Paul
from which rings the chime of ONE
              like OM.

—Josephine Carson

The Dwelling

50

Each lamp is fixed
on a window all its own.
Each shade is drawn
enough to see out but not in,
never blinking.
At this door a saucer of milk
is skinning over, at the next one
a shadow drains into the hall.
And the door they can all use,
with the letters painted backwards.

Each occupant poses unseen—
one readies a cake mix,
one secures a strip of wallpaper,
another is preparing for a test.
Each new digit on the clock
is a surprise, a beginning—
a reminder of all that's undone.
They wait for a buzzer or hinge. . .

The acceptance of steps
in a world not their own.

—Mark DeCarteret

Oft He Seems to Hide His Face

Singing so nobody thought they say
a song in out of tune and out of terror.
I asked his hurry why he was:
he stood in front of troubled doors,
his satchel black with ink-sick and misprinted
NY Times , and knocked with hoping hand.
His allocated misery was showing;
He closed his loud eyes to unanswer,
stood mulling in his minimal shoes
with minus soles, beyond the space
he occupied. His shirt writhed out
of the sick pants and lived apart,
while fractal creases multiplied his forehead.
Quiet as glass his traipse
commenced him into currents of the clock.
He rivered minutes while I under
all the subways sooted his soon coming.
When faced we handed down each other,
noses sniffly flaring everly.
The wrong dawn rose.

—Ben Passikoff

The Subplot

There's a dream where I die that repeats itself. Each time the death is different but the city recurs the same, modelled after every brick city I've been to. It is nothing like the West, though I insist on placing my dream in the West, & I am very much in love with it: old & falling apart into its narrow streets bricked up above the highway. Its sacred heart nods and no one is saved, necessarily, but some leave money & most at least light a candle at sunset. Each tree stands among the other shapes, diminishing, spotlit yellow, orange, red. The stars a big zero with nothing drawn inside, turning two dimensional, then black & white. The river turns into sand at the edge of the city and no one is saved, much less me, as my tin milagro legs nearly almost always fail at this turn. Slender comfort, my dream that is, collapsing to the pressures of the current dogma, to each violent thought I'd trade, if I could, for shoes or for toys. It is nothing, my dream, but I am in love with it and admit to the virgin of something with everyone, yes: we are all criminals, that for once we might recover from our wounds.

—Roger Hecht

EARTH

The snow laden branch
of the oak tree points
a bony finger to earth.

Ocamura summer:
in the barn two boys swing
over cut hay.

Sunday afternoon
by Jonathan Edwards' grave:
reading *The Age of Innocence* .

—John McEntyre

AIR

Antaeus Reflects from the Air

I don't much like it here, looking down
at the circular piece and patchwork
of Oklahoma, or Kansas maybe.
If the automobile deflowers the very
idea of distance (as Lewis says),

then the airplane completes the rape
altogether. Place falls off, dusty victim,
languid and abstract beneath the tumid
phallus of a white jet engine, accomplishing
its violation at almost infinite remove.

The cabin shakes. There is air
out there, once in a while a real
tornado. If Dorothy and Toto should
come by now in a clapboard house,
we might be able to call it home.

—Paul Willis

Accident

      Like a Minoan
bull-leaper he
flew in a sunny
arc under the green
leafed trees over
the hooded curve
of the car
bicycle flashing and
skittering down the street

      The boy shouted once
a high fierce
startle of spring
morning's cry
that death
in contest could
jump so high and far
so early on a
May morning

—Jeanne Nichols

The Parachutists

*"And let us remember the parachutists, emissaries from Israel,
who were the first to come to the aid of the nations besieged in
Europe, and who did not return."*
                    —Abba Kovner, Scroll of Fire

Well, it does not work like that.
Parachutists,
Shrouds over their heads,
Rehearse the sky.
Flak takes them, or bad wind.
We do not remember.
We do not always remember
Names of those we love,
Barely remember our ancestors
With faces like bad books
Long overdue, borrowed, or lost.
Yet, gliding thru clouddrift,
(One might see
Silk chrysanthemums,
Huge & fragile & stained)
Men & women risk everything
To land behind enemy lines
With faded documents,
Radio tubes & false names.
Tortured in strange countries,
They cry out loud & unheard.
Remember them?
We never knew their names.
We go through entire months
Without pausing in their honor.
Perhaps, that is what they wanted.
Certainly, it is what they died for.

                              —Louis Phillips

Bird Man's Siren Song

Do you look at birds
winged psyches souls a-flight?
Afternoons they pow wow high overhead,
commingle contrails, lazy eights,
          circle-squawk mandalas.

The dream of soaring unseen air is ours,
       coiling eddies, vortex swirls,
then dive
      dive
         dive eyedome fixed full yellow;
      lift-
   lift-
   lift-up   forward rush of wind
       dihedral wedge of wing
splitting, coursing air,
       winds buff as we rise and level,
         shoulders horizon-curved,
and dip thru red slivers of sunset,
       dark air held,
         palpable as spongy smoke;
       dawn held stroked warm by
quills that deck our fingers.

Take lead from currents,
        sprout wings.
       Why make arms?
re-open the chemistry of wings.

Let go
leave the ledge of bones;
       fearful to descend so quickly at first,
catch the self-made breeze
     of
       heat rising to you,
      the near perfect element
you are made for.

               —Robert Chianese

Choice

The mountain hasn't noticed yet
the clamoring. Bluejays,
hammering the important air,
are unreachable, too.

Shy-mouthed flowers prepare
to change color under the   sun
without question.

A girl has fallen off the mountain.
One step did not lead
to another.

Having neither wings nor roots,
we tremble in the chasm
of her plunge.

Choice opened the hole
she fell through,
but oh—the view.

—Norma Almquist

Spiders

The spider weaves her web.
I spin my sticky words
to catch the heart
of image, surprised
to trap such gracious prey
with music, the beat of blood.

She merely trusts her nature,
never suffers defeat
of wind or bigger nouns
that break her strands of home.
Spiders feed their progeny
fresh meat of art and storm.

My patterns change to serve
the space I choose. Like Spider
I was born with tools
for charting death and joy,
silky songs that praise the taste
and mysterious breath of bone.

—Mark Gibbons

In the Valley of the Loire

62

you see butterflies a-gasp on hollyhock and birds full-force in leafy canopy
a haze of heat thick on the sunflower fields a glimpse of tumbled
stone once a chateau this sky won't cease its postcard blue no matter
how it dazzles eyes that strain to see it all while body pedals up a hill
no wait! it's down a dale a hill again a dale a hill

then sweeping curves the river flat and wide to one side then the other
rides you over bridges old or new beneath which shelter boats at water's edge
somnolent fishermen at ease in shade don't even raise their eyes to see
a cyclist whistling by all pumping legs strong heart face glad
lungs full of blossom-scented air ears primed for a thrush-quick
song and inside quivering with *this* is how life can be and now is

—Annie Stenzel

Morning Walk

Things have a right to be
before they are made
to mean.

The scent of honeysuckle
on an April morning is
scent before it is
memory, and April is not
always the cruellest month.

A walk may be a journey
beginning, but first it must be
a walk, taken with pleasure,
without plan,

and a poem a vessel of
stillness, needing no
words beyond itself, no
comment but the bending
of a head over
the burning page
as if in prayer.

The ground is already holy
and the moment is its own
thanksgiving.

Suddenly in sunlight,
like the lift of a heron rising
from where you did not see him,
the world shifts, the frame slips
and all things once again
are made new.

Let them be new, then, while
the light lasts. Let joy
surprise you.
And when the veil lifts, refrain
even from the handmaid's question:
How can these things be?
Let them.

—Marilyn Chandler McEntyre

What is Manifest

64

in the air between the words
of a poem (on the page or
in mid-air between poet's
mouth and hearer's
ear) things you

hear with important parts
of what you are: the spleen
one day; a knee another; the sight
you saw, sometimes; often
your nose. You hear the piece
of hurt you thought had left
no smudge. There

in the space where a sound
leaves off, at a corner where
meaning turns to stretch
a limb or catch itself: a reaching
out envelopes you in what
you didn't know. Here

in the time it takes
the charge to pass from some
place infinitely close to one
beside it, far (as galaxies
go, but tiny) from where
we are. Now

—Annie Stenzel

Mind's Eye

What do you mean, do I know where we are?
It's you ahead of me; trusting you is
all my stripped and rubbled home could yield me,
and your day is night, your blindness and my
longing for my sons our mutual guides.
So we're all of us lost. Before you took
for granted the slow mists that are your eyes,
you say that you could see the curves of light,
the lay of squared, then devastated land.
You say you know the single cause of both.
Believe you? Maybe. The devastation
certainly. But order is as distant
from my mind's eye as sleeping next to you
each night, or as distant as one father
for all my sons, my wish that it were you.
You've never said what blinded you. And I
won't ask. Knowing this, your fingertips graze
the bit of vein between my hand and wrist:
thus led by you, awake and every night
yet to come is more than I ever hoped.
The touch convinces. I know where we are.

—Andrejika Beth Hough

Autistic

I know where he is, tonight.

There is no storm in the mountains, with
All of its colors and clouds to haul him off:
There is no looking for the first dry tip of
Green land for an abandoned Noah.

There is no counting the stars, the
Blinking eyes, the sour stones:
They are out there, but he is not.

I know where he is, tonight.

There are no locks and keys; both his hands
And mine are empty as a Houdini trunk:
There is no searching the thicket for fallen
Witches who have flown in from Egypt or Asia—

There is nothing but counting the blueness
As it holds above shuddering water.
There is nothing but knowing his heartbeat

As it climbs my arm, and rests at my shoulder.
He has no fear. His eyes are blue, and the moon is so white:

I know him.
I know where he is, tonight.

—Rhonda C. Poynter

Wake Up

You wake
and the sun throws
a pattern
on the fingery leaves
outside the window,
the shade left open
for morning light.
You didn't expect it
so yellow,
the leaves a cluster
of waxy peppers.
How gratefully you stare
and then it moves—
the beam,
a breeze—
and takes you.

—Robert Chianese

Hall Canyon / Soundings

eye takes its customary fill of lazy symmetries,
curve dance, slow ellipses,
four/four gavotte of whale backs and camels.
then hushed exhalations lick the ear;
soft, crackle-swishings of earth-bound wind,
curled sharpenings,
grass hiss, stalk clacks,
breathy takeoff of quail.

somedays windless hollows clang
a tenement racket of oil in harpoon pipes,
thud and drone of far-off ominous machines.

quiet rings its inner sounds:
we live in sinusoidal cradles of ancient pulses,
the solid amplitudes and frequencies of hills.
life secrets whisper here
in the spaced rise and fall of the heart.

—Robert Chianese

Morning Music

In shadows of waking dawn
Lakota love flute to lips
I play to the Tree People
watch the sun paint rainbows in a clouded sky.

Clear notes dance from my flute
drift across soft scented grass
spirals with lifting mist
to rest on leaves and flowers.

Turtle dove, high in maple tree   coos
sings a reply   imitates flute.
We join in music
and slip together into a world of harmony.

I float on a breeze
Light from Tree People souls guides me
through forests and meadows
over fast moving rivers and gentle streams.

To the soft coo flute
I sit in maple tree   listen
clear notes drift into morning's mist
reach the Tree People   me.

I coo-sing in greeting
she plays her music-voice
together we create
a duet.

—Mediha Saliba

Wedding Reception

70

This is a place for couples.
Generation vibrates in the air;
the old hide their bruises and stare,
bemused and wistful.

What of the uncoupled,
living out the final state -
the dailiness of it, the weight
of singularity held

like a third eye in the palm
to be opened at night,
in silence, in the raw light
of darkness. What is home

then? An outpost, a dry run,
an observatory whose lens
fumbles through space, sends
back signals begun

before the arc of coupling grooved
in the brain I/Thou.
Well. No matter. The I will plow
the earth, prow the grave

death boat in its sunken orbit.
To be alone is to include
the final solitude,
to make the end a habit.

—Norma Almquist

Last Breath

Streaming forth, a smooth, even column,
a corps of invisible cells, united
in a processional,
came to a singular cease.
No pause between breaths,
the rumored hiding place of enlightenment.

I lay unfilled, unbreathable.
So this is death,
a breath riding off as if I had no plans for it
to bear the promised blessing to my own true love
or to my deceiver the rattle of one last curse.
A slow little funeral all in itself.

But then above my outlaid form,
an inspiration and a letting go,
audible

—Charlotte Painter

At One

Neck pulled into high collar
she sits   writes
black hair tangled
eyes searching the lonely beach.

Nearby, sea gull clan
nestle into sand beds
bolster against wind
keep their distance.

Cold red fingers
jot word pictures
timeless   boundless, she
melds into grainy sand, salty mist, and ocean green.

Wind-spirit bends grasses flat
paints sand
erases stories of people, dogs, birds,
day visitors.

Lifting her head she finds
sea gulls
their obsidian eyes dance   know
accept.

—Mediha Saliba

Straw into Gold

Her hair was extremely exactly gold on the beach. She stole
the highlights
      off the glistening waves she dove into,
drew her hair through the surface and the light of the surface defracted
into her curls
      again and again she dove into the salty light
      and again came up and shook the water out of her eyes.
She brought all the sun's reflection back from the uncurled surf
      to the sand
      and lay on the heated mineral bed of the beach on a towel,
      a color of towel, and sparkled owning it all
I was ten eleven twelve, I owned none of it but what I saw she could
own,
      and practiced
combing light into my hair on the beach, sitting back
      in the dry dunes, wet ass of my one-piece clumping
      the sand under my thighs, I practiced tossing my lit hair
      in the tall marsh grass, taking up the scent of plumrose to
my little breasts   poking hard at the front of my suit
I followed her home at sunset to watch her barefoot on the summer
grass,
      spinning straw into gold on a moonlit lawn, the salty lawn
      crabgrassing toward the bank of sand
I followed her home off the beach, followed her tan toes, her tan back
      so lit with salt each downy hair a thread of light
      she brought from the water's edge

                —Mandy Richmond Dowd

Calgary in Winter

37 below
hands deep in down pockets
head covered in wool
I walk on snow   hard and crunchy,
    ice   too cold for fresh powder.
I rush along blanketed streets
    car heaters plugged in
    like horses to a hitching post
hurry around the park   not wanting to be out
but in need of movement.

Hair-strands thicken with ice
nose hairs freeze
frost bites face
stings eyes
strangles lungs.

Single maple tree   barren as all else
whispers   beckons.

With arms wrapped around rough bark
cheek pressed to uneven surface
tree-breath   thaws
gives life. Eternal Mother pulsates through limbs   warms

Across park's pink glow
Chinook rises   and
the soft kiss of snow descends.

—Mediha Saliba

Santa Barbara

Almost frost in the pines—
only fog in morning light.

Next exit, Santa Claus Lane:
always Christmas, never winter.

—Paul Willis

Hunger

In the morning a blanket of white—
first falling this year, and still falling
like my dream only it is the desert
and the wind carries silt creating a fine layer
over everything in the train car where I ride,
sun so hot I feel like a blanched almond,
still they say, "No windows, don't open
the windows: we must think of the food." I see
people around me gorging on figs, olives,
chunks of feta, fresh baguettes torn
easily between dark fingers. If I could breathe
I might think of food. I look
again at these passengers, crumbs stick
to the men's beards, juice sluices through the soft
folds of the women's chins. I move
to the doorway, push hard out
onto the platform between cars, take out a bag
of dago red and tilt tilt tilt. The sirocco blasts silt
onto my face, over the bota bag. My mouth fills
with the damp dog dust of Arènes de Nimes
on a late winter's afternoon; paella pots sizzle.
Six bulls slaughtered and I am famished.

—Marc Swan

Exposure

November winds tore through the trees
and your hands
and the substance of your love
fell on me
And the land jettied out in the tide.
Winter snowed a still, white quilt.

I took these pieces together
to bundle you in harbor,
though nothing stays inside the safety
of love, and nothing stays
the rocking still for long.
Always a wind hollows through.

And your hands, and the substance you are
have landed me in this
rough ground—
here are the brown eyes of your clarity,
here the brown, brown of your moods

Always a wind, and the rooting trunks of trees
in the city squeeze for life
the soil beneath
the tar, and concrete, and cars, and you
pass the water to me

—Mandy Richmond Dowd

Early February

This is a sad, grey time—
pleasure here and there, but little
that deepens into joy—
not even grief that drives the soul
to utter its *de profundis*
and so be widened into prayer.

Only the feeling of nothing to rise to:
neutered moments of waiting, wanting
something, not knowing
what.

Laundry to be done and breakfast
cleared away.

Grace doesn't always come as a rainbow.
Sometimes it hovers like a pewter sky
tucked in around the treetops,
bringing the landscape close to the eye.

Still, grace comes on a day like this
in odd disguises:
traction on my boots,
the man chipping ice off the library steps,
fat truck tracks to drive in—

and all the shades of grey.

For the gifts of greyness let us give thanks:
cobblestones and flagstones and boulders of granite,
clapboard houses, dark-shuttered and lamplit in the afternoon,
snow on asphalt,
pencil and charcoal,
the naked stretch of steel that protects us at the bridge's edge,
old movies from a kinder time,

the wolf and the owl—hungry and hidden—
the rabbit's fur,
the hawk's eye,
the dolphin's back,
the cocoon where a caterpillar
quietly works out
its salvation.

—Marilyn Chandler McEntyre

Other Cruel Months: February (in California)

Defiant among the anytime
odors of the city a waft of early
Spring crashed in
the open window
Sat by my sleeping face until
its presence could not be ignored.

I swallowed gallons of it before I could
defend myself; had to
haul my scent-drugged body
up off the floor, cross the room, and
slam closed the window.

—Annie Stenzel

Where he Lived and What He Lived For

"Worked all my life for Pacific Lumber."
He held up crooked fingers, calloused hands.
"Grew up in Bandon on the Oregon coast."

"He liked to watch the storms," his wife put in.
"Most people wait to comb the beach, not Fred."

He raised a rugged smile. "No TV.
To see a real sou'wester, feel it come,
be down there with it, I thought that was somethin'."

—Paul Willis

The Wind

Tip the locks of a towhead child
his hands held up in bliss
to greet his Mother and Father.

Blow the dust from the dying in the street
their blood stepped over another statistic
of lost souls.

Bend the boughs of a dogwood tree
golden leaves fall, then dance and swirl
in pursuit.

Clear the smoke from bombed villages
let children see the sky pray
humanity might wake up soon.

Cool summer days in valleys of cement
when dry heat
ripples across concrete in desert mirages.

Chill nights in mountain lodges
where lovers gather beside fireplaces sip wine
make love.

 Unseen you weave into and through Life.

—Mediha Saliba

One Moment

80

Crashing waves beat shore   foam
blows across beach where wild-grasses bend flat
and sand ripples erase footprints.
Salt-wind bites   stings eyes and
sea gulls make shadows   hover.

Two arm lengths away grays and whites
balance on currents
chest feathers quiver in gusts
curious eyes watch
caw-voices call   call   call.

I spread my arms in laughing imitation
feel wind wrap, smell sea   forget all else
        fly with gulls.

—Mediha Saliba

5th Floor, Rear
Near Varick Street, NYC

They have spread a net over
The airshaft rear,
And where my mother and
Her sisters, chary
Fishmongers' wives all and born
On the other side,
Where they
Once called out to each other and
Where they
Watched for their husbands'
Carrier birds to come home
(Could the men be far behind?) and
Where they
Reeled in sooted laundry still
Stinking of mackerel

In this slice of air now

The co-op board makes arrangements
To trawl dead pigeons.

My mother's baby sister, last rent-payer,
Watches the net weigh down, past her eyes
Looking out the window;
She pinches her nose shut
With an old clothespin.

She tells me all of this,
Breathing only through her mouth.

—Andrejika Beth Hough

Object Lesson

82

Beneath the
             DON'T
             WALK
             sign
this transient
stands
like public art
the city
wants removed
A breeze turns
the pinwheel
he holds
inches
from his face

—Erik Anderson-Reece

Notes from a Leaky Life

They can take me away, all of me, and still
I would remain.
Life is an easel
you lean your best against. It is a fence
and pickets knock loose and dogs get through.
Pet the dog when it licks you, pet the dog
for its long pink tongue.

If the gate is hinged with a spring,
your coming and going will sound with a clap.

Clap, here. Clap, gone.

(These are things to remember.)
It's ten o'clock and your tea's gone cold:
Listen to the grass
as it grows through the fence.

The tilt-a-whirl in the wind
is your mind: take a ride.
Disembark on the soft cloud of your lungs letting out.

—Mandy Richmond Dowd

Reach, Reach, Reach

for the stones are a belt around your waist
and you are walking through a wood
and the darkness is the forest and overgrowth
of your thinking for nothing good But the sound
of life in the trees will be the life in your head & let it
be enough for now, the sound of life in the trees

—Mandy Richmond Dowd

There is More Than This Out There

84

More than the eyelids clumping down. We have watched the iris dilate at the morning fog; watch we now the bones sinking under the bay. This is the body you transport and in whose care we come. Drink me the winter morning, drink me up every capillary: like rum, the promise of my presence.

Do I repeat myself for your sweet sake? Do I say the same and the same? Have I not predicted the coming of your what? You lose me now, the loose thread, fine as a web in your fumbling fingers.

Who are you in the mirror when you wake? When did you last look and ask? Is this I or me or a group inhabiting, or is this vacancy reading lights . . .

Come in, sit down and make yourself. This is the city and all the roofs are wet with (count them) lives transposed to a busy key. In five time and eight time, and you come with a waltz. Whose hand do you hold in the dance?

—Mandy Richmond Dowd

After a Visit to the Musée des Beaux Arts

Above these Brussels clouds somewhere
the moon is full, she knows: it says so
on the calendar. A normal night here, though,

defies moon-watchers. Craning her neck
in an attic room, nervous in the cool
air surging through the open window, watching

a place where the moon might be, she sees
in an instant some clots of cloud are parted
by the wind—the night transforms itself and

This is the sky Magritte saw: Moon
suspended from a tree limb, city
inattentive, sprawled below. The breeze

has made for loud leaves that
lash the branches they're attached to,
slap wet window panes, cast images inside

to spin in shadows vivid on
white walls. But just as it wasn't all
Magritte saw that he showed her, so

the night and its attendant moon
had more to say than she had
heart or will to hear

—Annie Stenzel

Entranced
—*for Kathleen, and her brother*

She was making the unlikely comparison
between New York City and the Milky Way,
and so waved her hands round in a vortex
that described the physics of the Big Bang,
or the style of a dancer. It showed the way
in which our lives circle in on one another,
how vast metropoli spring and spiral forth.

One loses sight of the other—that was
our point—how you'd never recall
there's yet this cosmic mumbo-jumbo
up above the skittering masses encased
in concrete burrows. Putting one foot
in front of the next, you forget to look up.

You so often have to get to some place else,
Sonoma County or Martha's Vineyard,
to know how the night sky can still be seen
or sense how far we go and short we are.
But we'd each come our little distances
from our small-town Wyoming roots.

Now when I recall that stellar arc still
wheeling out, past imagination, I know it's
Cheyenne's other poet who first spoke about
getting unlocked from the urban trance.

—Sharon Page

AIR

Spiders at school
spin webs that connect
each leaf.

Reading and writing,
I'm showered by
leaves from autumn wind.

Nearly new moon
seen through moving clouds:
thoughts of a distant friend.

—John McEntyre

WATER

Young Wife on the Ark

The clutter, the noise, the stench, those three—
Oh, and the rain—if I could be free
Of those four things I'd be all right.
My headaches would stop.
I'd be able to sleep.
I haven't had a breath of fresh air
Or closed my eyes in weeks.
Everything's wet. Everything stinks.
I'd faint and die if I went downstairs
But even here, in the galley, it reeks.
Odors of camel and parrot and sheep
Have curdled the last milk left in my breast
And the baby screams a mute protest
Scarcely heard through the clatter of leaks.
Each day gets darker, each night the lamp
Burns a little bit lower; there's less fit to eat.
Mildew has rotted the melons and wheat
And the yams have sprouted beards of white hair
Like his beard, old man's, kneeling there
Chin on the porthole. He tells us we're saved.
The others believe him. But I've heard him pray.
And I pray along with him through the dull day:
I pray that the panthers will spring on the apes
I pray the lions will kill the gazelles
I want the snakes to devour themselves
I'd like the turtles to choke in their shells.
I'd choke them myself if I still trusted violence.
I don't. It does nothing. God himself tried to silence
The world with a rainstorm, a brainstorm that failed.
His tantrum helped no one; we're still lost, still jailed
In a dark little ark where captive beasts pace
Back and forth in their own filth forever.
Dry-eyed at high-tide, I lie awake
My baby a stranger, a stranger my mate,
I'm told there will soon be an end to this flood.
And what then? I wonder. Mud. And more mud.

—Molly Giles

Boy and Pregnant Mother
Aquatic Beach

He has dragged her here, sea-heavy
blissful barge of his salt nights
to the shore of their first watery fill.
Sea-rooted, pillared in foam
she stares out. He dives and
bursts up, eyes streaming before her
sweep and swirl of green dress,
adoring her naked foot
in the lurch and swell under her own
billowing held hump where
his brother or
his sister-to-be swims.
He leaps with the wind and circles,
wrapping her ankles in
dark weed.
His wind-warped shouts rocket
around her. His starfish fingers
lightly claim their catch
one last time.

—Josephine Carson

Boys on the Beach: Jersey Shore

92

Knees scraped, skinny calves poking
through frayed, cut-off denim,
they dance a ballet
choreographed by broiling sand.

Salt-caked lemon-pepper hair,
freckled shoulders, skin of
Italian cherry-ice, they
bear their badges of office —
       five and dime snorkels and
       styrofoam surfboards,
       blue-speckled, brand new.

They sail past me
smelling of low tide,
Coppertone and inflatable balls.
In their shouts I hear
seagulls or sometimes
the rush of crested waves.

—Colleen Lindsay

Dream by the Sea

My father, in life,
was a disappointed man.
Slowly, wave after wave,
our feet sank in the sand.

I had to confess to him
that for all my schemes
I had little then to show.
His white hair blew in the breeze.

I listened to my father
until the tide and he were one.
And by and by I listened more
until the waves sighed with faint praise.

—Craig Taylor

Where Did it Go

from the end to the end?
Short life
live a quiet vigilance,

count the pebbles on your walk, soft
spots between your toes

Behind the split light
where the epileptic eyes turn in
there is the still of the sea sick sea

This is the empty-breasted sailor's dream:
That his locker
will open into sand
and give him free
of holding

And these the sinks of caps of waves,
That waiting never offers richer time
That patience is the pretense of the self that doesn't dare

away with you then
into fields of swirly weed
& salt bended eye

Try trust as if your heart were so
wide as the mouth of a boathouse

What does your brain do on its dance
looking left and left then right then left?
Where did it go, the light in the tidal sea?

—Mandy Richmond Dowd

Some Crickets

The river bank is like this: kites can only fly
as far as their strings. We walk on the edge of the water;
sidewalks are too permanent for dusk.
Here we and the warm earth will remember our footprints.

This is a dance that we have learned to do;
one step back and two steps forward, finding our way one smile at a time,
we drift across the bridge and back.
Maybe the journey is the whole point:
I pick blades of grass and tie them in knots.

Sunset is also a bridgewalker, taking fast gliding steps into the water,
dropping flames of laughter and impermanence around her beckoning feet.
Every spark matters only because it is beautiful,
and only if we are watching it—
sometimes we are watching each other instead.

We pass gates of wrought iron vines that smell like barbecues:
it is spring. Twenty people fell into the river this morning.
I didn't know then what this would be like, and I still
don't know the names of the flowering trees,
but I know your fingers remember my hand
And I know there are crickets and singing cicadas behind us,
and also ahead of us.

—Mary Teichert

WHERE ICARUS FALLS

At the dedication of the Chicago Locks: September 14, 1938

96

Control the river, sluice it, wash it through
The locks Chicago hired you men to run:
Wet men all: you my husband, brothers, son;
Long after Father worked the great lake, you
Men built your locks; this made him one who knew
The river as it knew itself. Undone,
It was reversed, suckling Lake Michigan.
Father, key man, knew this. He knew me, too.

This can't be. Way before they built the locks,
The river sluiced out typhoid. As for me,
I bind my hair, scared run from my men's docks
Secured, though, to my insecurity.
But water as it's rising, falls; thus rocked,
My hair and Father's river tumble free.

—Andrejika Beth Hough

To Tell You

You can't step into the same river twice,
but I'd like to. I need an audience
for the things I want to show: someone needs
to want to see. It's possible that no one hears
the tree, falling in the forest near only
two teenagers who will never confess the Chevrolet
and the darkness and a lot of other things:
Does it make a noise? Do I?
Everything always boils down to love. And so
I splash in again and again: repetition
versus development. Sometimes you don't know
why I say this again. And I will;
I'll take the fatal plunge every hour 'til I make you
look. Make you hear me: hey! I love you still.

—Mary Teichert

Augustine's Bridge

Amor meus pondus meum
—St. Augustine

My love my weight, this night I am traveling
across the wide river of what can't be said,
looking down into reflected stars.

Held up like this, by hope, I feel my life
grow simple as this span of words, articulate,
declarative, as if all the myriad

knots tied by will and the lone intelligence
had suddenly come free, along with the questions
I no longer need answers for.

How they used to crowd around, the questions,
as hungry creatures come clamoring to the hand,
passionate to be touched and fed.

—Karen Fiser

Swimming in the Light
—for Mary Oliver

We splashed into your poems like children
at the water's edge, dove
into them, delighted, almost afraid to open
our eyes.

Words like fish caught the sun and turned
it to shocking turquoise, gold, red
like the fire in the opal, silver
like the curl of breakers at midnight.

We rode each poem like a wave.
Again and again we came
to rest, bellies in the sand, and rose
laughing, and crying, "One more!"

He plunged, then I plunged, following
each other like dolphins at play until
we paused, and dove into the last poem
side by side.

There was no one watching from the shore to keep
life guarded.

This is what truth feels like:
Light, like an ocean buoys
us up and we are
surrounded, immersed, astonished,
completely loved.

For a moment we remember:
      we are the light.
      We are the water
           and all the little fish
           dance in our bones.

You carry us homeward. We reach
for one another: he and I and the poem
are one
until, borne on the final swell, you leave us
gasping on the shore.

—Marilyn Chandler McEntyre

Prospering (Continuous Present)

100

1
Hours in the well
and the rising damp

The trunk of the Madrone holds out
a wet arm firm
in the night as in the day

The hour is a hand in the dark

2
Too much to know, too much
let it go into the deep and shifting planes of rain
Chase the taste
of life up from the dirt
Leave the many twisted meanings deep
to compost and turn under late summer late

August is a hamper   throw her your dirties
Early spring come clean

3
Out of the silence then, all that's left:
the head of a bulb on the bones
pressing open from the lobes
the swell, a sound itself cracking in the ears
listen to the sound of honey in the limbs
that's honey in the limbs, to you
honey where the sun seeps in and rain
plays on a thirsty skin
honey in the deep columnar well
gold in the dark and the hand
gold in the hand of the heart

4
Down the river of veins
the shores are peopled with love
Bruises tell of floods but oh
the plenitude of beginnings unended

Pain will take you down, the body bend you
but at the banks, there in the curves
of the jointed turns the tides
will tumble, there the changes are learned

—Mandy Richmond Dowd

On Searching Through a Taoist Medical Treatise

If I didn't have a personal body, what vexations would I have?
—Tao Te Ching

101

Imagine that your backbone is a river.
Send for the void and contemplate heaven.
To be sure the body gods stay together,
drink water left outside in the light of the moon

on the 15th of the month. Remember that the bear
always accompanies fear, water, cold,
and cracking joints, while the tiger
goes with metal, lungs, sorrow. Hold

the child all dressed in red in the crimson
palace of your heart. Concentrate. He will descend
to the lower cinnabar field, to make you live long.

Master Redpine, Minister of Rain under Shennong,
directs all who hope to leave their pain behind,
Stay a little longer each day in oblivion.

—Karen Fiser

Feedings

Green-headed striped gray mallards
crimple the slow-moving waters
in their last stretch as river
before the precipitous falls.

Flapping flocks thicken the shore
waiting their turn for a peck
at the seeds flung out over the snow
by a neighbor massaging the belly

of her old setter prone at the feeder:
*He'll be OK. Just gets these attacks
in the winter.*   Sure enough, he's up,
tail wagging my way back from the mailbox—

a bit after breakfast.

—Edwin Honig

WATER

Santa Cruz Island

103

The path from Scorpion Cove slants up the ridge
through mustard, coastal sage, and wild oats,
and finds a grassy upland where we sat,
all circled in the green and gold of May.
The wind blew billows through our salted hair,
the grasses pointing east across the blue
to Anacapa, mounted in the sky.

Schoolchildren we, and parents, and our guide
described the Chumash and their rainbow bridge
that arched from Santa Cruz to mainland lost
in haze beyond the channel, how they stepped
across the colors, hoping soon to reach
new oaks and peaks, but curious looked down,
just as their goddess warned them not to do,
and fell like Icarus into the waves.
And thus came dolphins, brothers to the tribe.

We looked out from our headland, seeing still
the span of crimson-violet and the flight
of strong brown bodies entering the sea,
glistening now with fins upon their sides
and leaping to regain the footing lost,
and arching back in silvered play of light.

We looked save one of us—lips pursed, a man
with wrinkled brow who stood and stared apart
outside our circle, back upon the path.
Instead of wind, he held up to his ear
a shining shape no bigger than a shell
and spoke to it in bursts. For him there was
no need of rainbows, nowhere to look down.

But he was one. The rest of us arose
and climbed the track to middens of white shell,
the aftertaste of abalone feasts
high on the hill beside the sun, or stars,
where hands swim through the air in fading light,
still dripping with belief, with nourishment.

—Paul Willis

Dreaming

104

Beneath Persimmon tree's hanging boughs
I watch giant gold fish
pretend they are coy.

In graceful pods they swim
mouths open wide to receive morsels
tossed by me.

Silly creatures growing large and fat
only to be snapped up
by a blue heron   such foolishness.

Not for me.
My world is reality   concrete and formed
no illusion here.

A dragonfly joins my quiet repose
On scalloped lotus leaf,
wings of dragon scales glow iridescent in the afternoon sun.

Eyes too large for its head
he skims the water   me
and hums of times gone by   when

dragons took to the sky, breathed fire and fear,
but now transformed
speak of dreams.

And while I gaze at my reflection
a koi touches the surface
ripples dance out   expand.

—Mediha Saliba

Buena Vista
  —for Willy Rust

Lodgepole, white pine
shine as if a sun
were setting inside each one.
A man, a girl, a boy stand
at lakeshore with poles at ready,
feet lost in showy banks of snowbrush,
of mountain heather. They hardly see
the cirque of granite, bowl of red-

stained snow about them, evening
sky that promises a day again
as blue as many days gone by.
There are worries, yes, as few
and as invisible
as mosquitoes hovering in air, sure
to thicken as night falls, but now
a nuisance easily repelled

by the sudden word:
"I got one! I caught one!"
The man traverses patiently
to girl or boy and he agrees,
"Yes, a big one. Very big."
The fish is fingered, barb
removed from bloody lip, gills
stroked—the trout released

back into the clean cold.
It fins away, bearing our sins
in its aching mouth, another
ichthus, all that we need
for a coming of darkness
as three lines arch and reach
and fall across the glint again
in pleasant places.

                              South Yosemite
                              —Paul Willis

Litany

Body of water before me, its edge
at my feet   I say to myself Don't jump! things will surely
get better   Body of water before me, autumn
leaves in its shallows with tadpoles   A squiggle
of watery sun on the surface that barely
moves there is no breath, no wind
Body of water before me of course
I won't jump; I have shoes
on   the sun a warm hand
at my shoulder   slight scent
of the tree Benjy said Caddy
smelled like   but this isn't
a novel   Body of water before me
that tree a willow in springtime will drag
lissome branches across
the body of water before me where
there is no disappearance from pain into
the body of water before me not a lake
or the sea not a river   a pool   a lagoon   only a pond

—Annie Stenzel

Above San Pablo Bay, 1993

I confess, readily,
that I am moved too much by sorrow,
even sorrow for trees cut down
for a market soon out of business.

Sorrow is relative
for boys not quite men
who pilot their skateboards
in the new-found territories
of abandoned asphalt.

And what of the wild, darting egret,
fishing nearby, in the estuary,
as the flags of the world steam by?

In July, jellyfish from the Black Sea
hitchhiked into San Pablo Bay.
Out of work, I walked to the water
and watched the jellyfish open and close
like small, fancy cocktail umbrellas.

—Craig Taylor

Live Your Life as it Is

108

This will change, this too
like everything else.
Will come, will go.

Here is the middle of a dark life
: You in it, you in it

The earth itself never holds still
how stuck can you be?

Sit in the avalanche
your heart will know

ask for no one
but your wholeness
while your hand is in the motion of life

moving into its own
gentle, breathing center

toes are a wonder
a free thing
every word worth the labor of repetition

until you understand
        what a free thing
                it is

Follow the tide, push and pull, plush and pill,
on the crabby ocean bottom

into coral into eel grass into the
thick of the whole heart you are,
you silly wonder of a human
heart, eyes as wide as walnuts in a bowl

In the hollow of your
sketch like a brain
you will be watched

make it up
as you go

—Mandy Richmond Dowd

Dear Sir

Maybe, maybe not.
This letter could turn to ashes before
I am through. It is that

I want you to stand out here
in the rushing narrows of the unknown
where the life pushes, pushes

Don't beg in the sands for a fancy
to buoy you through the fright
of the pressing unknown

You have a feeling / I have
a feeling / today
I will die, die dead as a bark

run aground / today
I feel the crumbling
of my hull / good

today I feel fine
about that / today we are free
to look at outlooks

today my feelings assure me
this difficult time will pass / today, nothing
you say feels real

each day you borrow the fancy a feeling lends
truth is in and is
immediate, intractable, more

than what may be which flutters
in the offing
Truth is here

in the extreme of here
in the extreme
of our discomfort

in the vast unanswerable
questions, here and only
here at last our hearts unbound

—Mandy Richmond Dowd

Alyana, Turkey
Wednesday, September 23

        The rose-colored boat
with its shark's jaw reflection
in the early blue of the harbor
the water old and still
the blue and red and pink and white
fishing boats ready to go
nets piled
Active and understandable
men doing understandable things
with engines and lines and oars   things
they've always done

        The shops with their recognizable
blouses and sandals and tablecloths and
onyx ashtrays

        The men, solemn over their glasses
of morning chai, sugar lump and tiny spoon
ceremonial under the vine leaves

        But the rose-colored boat
waiting in the harbor—

        If we lived here we might
sail out of the harbor
leaving our balcony and plants
and the white curtains blowing
under the strange and intimate
stars

                                —Jeanne Nichols

The Boat

The sad wooden boat aches in its keelson
to be ruinously drunk, to be something
other, as it drifts, hollow, too full
of itself, out from the averted shore.
If only for the sleek fish to pout
and roll up under the boards of the bottom
as a cat purls beneath the outstretched legs
of its foolish, grateful master, the widow
with her gray book of services. To be
the widow, just then convinced she sees
through the eye of the smallest particulate
the convex breadth of the first world,
the grasses in sunlight paring cheerfully back
for a path lined by white stones and curling up
over the hill in a parabola of God
and cat's tail.

                              If only for moonlight,
to annihilate the stuffed gulch of clouds,
as the moon once did, the young, sleeping boat
at midlake, walking as a man alone
on a frigid road who quickly turns to find
what it was on his shoulder—and then the fear,
realizing it was the delirious photons
of moonlight to which he'd at last opened.
To know that man's same fear
the night his wife could not stop opening
into herself, her taste, the first minute
and the elegant alabaster surprise
of the second, and then her tears and the high
feathered weeping he heard over her breasts
as she entered the third, and then finally
the last human silence of her fourth, and on,
flooding into him . . .

                              Long ago the young boat
had stirred under the full face, risen
over the mountain, beaming the narrow white walk
over the fearful water. A thick wind rose

(cont.)

in consent. The lake sent each distinct runnel
of itself crosswise through the walk
as the still boat stared—and knew
this was to be the great moment
of staying still. The moment of nothing
mattering. And then . . . nothing
came of it, no light spilled away
from the perfect hyaline lake
the boat had always imagined.
It wanted to see at the margins
of its own surface not the gunnels, but
the shaped wooden planks, then the varnish
giving way to striations of deep streaks
on light, the streaks giving way to terrain,
maps, numbers, and finally to itself.
A last memory of planks in the wind.
Then—just the wind.
                              But dawn had turned
the boat out again, lost as a young husband
before the morning his pregnant wife, fast
from the geneticist, stands outside
his open office, offering a pink
or blue rose over the threshold. And so,
of course, tonight the sad boat longs
to be that man, too, not for the moment
when he lays the fool flower across his arms,
nor when he sees in its inward face
two dazzling children skipping the old path,
nor for just after, when he sweeps
the floating woman into the room and they stare
at each other and repeat one name slowly. No.
Rather, for the moment just after that, his wife
leaving, cheery, an abundant red sail
down the hallway, and he, buoyant, certain,
an immaterial empty bowl pressed upon the water.

—Kevin Clark

Hall Canyon / Twelve-thousand-year-old Shells

113

Broken shells,
  unfossilized,
  dust the hillside
with brittle lace.

Did someone dump them here —
  old clam pit,
  Adam's midden,
cache of worn out glyphs?

From the canyon's fresh mouth
  debris flows
  silted their offshore beds,
muds upon muds.

Pressed, jolted, lifted, scrambled,
  they ride the tectonic coaster.
  Waters bury them;
flakes flow from cut seams.

Asleep in this deep
  will I wind up so scattered,
  or, like the clay-stuffed shell
the dark rock encased, stay intact?

And who would puzzle out
  in care-shaped words
my life from well-kept bones?

Better join the hillside litter,
  abstract bleached adornings,
  shattered, spread calcium art,
mineral silent, re-forming.

—Robert Chianese

Antediluvian Baseball

114

One night, all the bases came to visit
home plate. While frogs croaked
in the outfield they floated in the batter's box
like lily pads, getting a sense
of where it happened.

Two ravens landed on the pitcher's mound
and called for blood. Aluminum bleachers
began to buzz with St. Elmo's fire, ecstatic.

Then the rain came and told secrets
about antediluvian baseball, how Abel
made it all the way in on a sacrifice,
how Noah saved the best pitchers
but left the umpires to drown.

—Paul Willis

WATER

The stately egret stretches,
steps, stretches, pauses,
then dives deeper.

The otter rides
on his back without motion:
now and then he claps.

By the waterfall
the sparkles glisten
for less than one second.

—John McEntyre

FIRE

Sierra Says

118

Mosquito says, remember me.
Stream says, willow, willow.
Lake says, leap trout.

Meadow says, shooting star.
Snow says, suncup.
Granite says, old bones.

Glacier says, bergschrund.
Cloud says, thunder coming.
Sun says, sun says, sun says it all.

—Paul Willis

FIRE

Lumen

119

At Sol's center light consumes its own dark rays
heat/light/motion meld and bubble timespace chunks
beyond Dante's concentric dreams.

Hydrogen shimmies to Helium
"H" to "H-e" blows out blips
threehundredsixtythousandmiles to surface
on their way to oblivion—
neutrino
neither neutral nor darling
threading whatever matters
on colorless wings
the ninetythreemillionmiles to earth.

Deepest caves
hold off light
and parts of light
so dark the watchman cannot see
the water tank neutrino cuts
its trace, its being there.

Cold, silent-dark his station,
spaces dense against the bared intensities
at sun's core.
What patience hides his glooms?
What glories will he sing
when his long night breaks?

Note: Neutrinos are massless, electrically neutral particles within the nucleus of
an atom; they are emitted during radioactive decay, as when hydrogen changes to
helium, fueling stars; they penetrate most substances. Scientists search for traces
of neutrinos in water tanks in deep caves; they appear very infrequently.

—Robert Chianese

Transcript

120

She looks scrawny and peaceful,
the young nun in blue jeans,
like the other two passengers,
like we do now, I think.

We're wedged between soft sacks
on top of a cargo truck
in the middle of Africa.

Right now, only thorn trees reach for us.
The red dust of the track
swirls up.

Baboons in clusters scatter
as we plunge along.
A giraffe stares through beige branches.

The five of us loll and dip
with the potholes,
share mangoes and sip
from our sacred water bottles.

Dry sweet air, mango flesh,
rough hemp sacks leaking millet,
our own soft, spaced words . . .

Who we are disappears
into light and movement,
into scent and touch.

—Norma Almquist

House Fire

Fire and water
are not so dissimilar.
Both offer life generously
and jealously snatch it away; both sway
to their respective and inexplicable tides, surging
and ebbing, leaving changes strewn about
as do the most careless and ironic of gods.

Fire and water both
baptize us in the difficult,
bathe us in mortality, scour our souls clean of security,
christen us in fragility, warn us
that our proper element is earth, and to earth all things return.
A drop, a spark, a cry of warning,
a moment of time more or less
added to the fateful equation,
makes us all philosophers of the subtle, of the "what if";
slams our lives up against those tiny, perilous distinctions—
between the sweet seas of fluid our cells swim in
and the wave that draws the sated mouth under;
between the warm circle of the yellow winter hearth
and the summer pyre that devours all our yesterdays.

—C.A. Prettiman

Funeral Objects

122

The Chimney remains, a mockery
of comfort. Stone is always solitary
no matter what grows near,
always the survivor . . .

                  Nothing is so hungry
as fire. It ate the house,
the immediate family. Who will wear
the funeral mask? Only curiosity
marks the end and a friend
going through the motions of salvage:
here, the charred money box;
all around, the estate of vague divisibility.
Three generations come down
in an hour's worth of rubble and ashes
for lawless nourishment in wood,
twisted permutations in brass,
a swill of mirrors.
In one huge breath, like the birth
roar of the planet, it broke
enigmas on the master bedroom,
delicacies everywhere,
the children . . .

                  Somewhere else
in carnival season laughing children
eat skulls made of sugar, playing
at death and living out unspoiled dreams.

—Lahna Diskin

The Books We Miss

When I got back from my run this morning, new snow
dusting the ridgetop, I found you lying face-down
on the living room floor. "Dad," you said, "It's terrible.
Somebody burned down the library. Some lady
did it. All those Tintin books—they're gone."

Tintin for you. For me it was the pair of novels
I had given just last month. The librarian had made
a fuss, set them out at eye level on the paperback rack.
I couldn't bear to think of them now, crumbling
and charred, the stand a twisted sculpture of sorrow.

Just yesterday I learned they were going
out of print. This lady, she didn't have to rub it in.

—Paul Willis

Wildfire

*"The river reflected whatever it chose of sky and bridge and
burning tree, and when the undergraduate had oared his
boat through the reflections they closed again, completely,
as if he had never been."*
                        —Virginia Woolf, *A Room of One's Own*

Ten months ago,
After wildfire scoured the little peninsula—
Leaving ashen soil, smoldering trunks
And rusty withered foliage—
Only khaki water showed something near green.

I thought that color would be forgotten forever,
But already a fresh explosion
Rises like an Irish Isle from the lagoon
(Pewter-dull now by comparison).
Waves of weedy blooms—oxalis and mustard grass—
Run up the bank and over the hill in a
Lemon yellow memory of fire.
The usual cormorants perch on stumps,
Hanging their charry wings out to dry.
A migratory duck carves a "V" through the water.

Twenty times each academic quarter, this being the nineteenth,
I come upon a lone white egret,
Statuesquely stalking the same crescent shallows.
The bird cocks a golden eye at my motion, then away,
Remembering only what is necessary.

                        —Carla Mengel

Seven-Step Program

1
Purple sage, meadow, morning,
Red-winged blackbird rides a perch
on yellow mustard, rides another,
swaying, calling: *I have found it,
          I have found it.*

2
A trail, a ledge, a buzzing rattler,
fat and folded in his coils. No room
for both of us. I climb below, regain
the path beyond. Kind of him
to sound a warning, say goodbye.

3
Oak limb crashes in the forest,
merges with the sound of sun
in afternoon. I hear for all
the absent people, walking,
sleeping, in other canyons.

4
Alder roots and tendrils reaching
down to water. Trout are waiting in
the rapid. Long and patient
fishing, this—the wetting and the
slow release of many lines.

5
Wind all night, moon
and then bright stars,
a planet, glowing
like the Coulter pine cones
lost in embers at our feet.

6
Small snow taps
the tent at dark, spats
of ice from Jeffrey pine.
Mist, fog coming where
the bear drop over the rise.

7
After fire, manzanita
waving arms like wailing
women. Wet green
under the roots, wallflower
re-imagining the flames.

San Rafael Wilderness
—Paul Willis

Penn Valley

This morning I run the dirt levee
that holds the irrigation ditch.
Levee and ditch together
make a contour line, dry and wet,
across the side of the low ridge.
Levee and ditch and water and I
pass new homes dug here
and there in hard red earth,
sifted for gold and left for dead
a hundred forty years ago.
A jackrabbit bounds like a deer
into the cover of manzanita,
red-tailed hawk sifting quiet
among charred oaks.

Fires, not people, live here best.
There is warning in the hot sweet
of blackberries stifling the air,
in the shrill of the hawk
in a blackened pine.
The largest houses crown
the ridge on naked platforms,
hoping to rest on air alone.
Through porticoes and picture windows
they will have the finest views
of sweep and scorch of conflagration,
and when they catch they will shine
like beacons, sending the message
from hilltop to hilltop that the invaders
have come again.

—Paul Willis

Tragedy as Redemption

I know the (cleansing?) fires of clinically perfect
disasters;
the larger flames purging
(suffering being inescapable)
my bible conscience;
I know the shifting
(This is
giving
me
depth)
crumbling of a seemingly minor earthquake,
threatening the suddenly precarious
sidewalks of my surreal world
(step on a crack, break

And I know
about Growth; and I know
about Salvation; and I know
(now)
about Tragedy as Redemption
but I don't know
if I can
bear
this much

grace.

—Mary Teichert

The Creation of the Abyss

128

And yet, someone's got to keep
civilization going. Adam
and a Mediterranean earth goddess

did their part: produced two sons
in the hyacinth nights after Eden,
warm by the Tigris river, her body

fit rib-close to his.
There is no lack of void
around our timeless kiss;

we have stepped into the abyss. The closed
economy of our fall is all we have . . .
I am dying, Egypt, dying!

The seventh sorrow is a slow goodbye, yet
abandon me now
and the drops that we have bled together

will be the same red as any other apple;
our story a domestic tragedy.
The despair of the universe

dwindles and it seems
this brave new world is only a broken
olive branch, and my wings begin to burn:

and for what?

—Mary Teichert

Burned at the Stake

Heretic martyr, chained to the stake, Jan Hus sang
and prayed while a hooded executioner held a torch
to the dry sticks that pricked his feet
and a sober crowd watched, waiting

for what? An act of God? A shriek of pain? A promise
to recant? Shadrach's angel to return
on special assignment? Or only the grim relief taken
in another's torment: this time, thank God, it's someone else's turn?

The mystery of faith may baffle the reasoning
mind no more than the lively maze of sensing
nerves, rushing glands and beating brain. Pain
foreseen hardens muscles into armor, charges

the senses and lets some wild thing loose
in the only animal able to imagine
its own death or amplify its pain
with possibility. Did he wonder, I wonder,

what would come first—suffocation by smoke
or the searing lick of flame on fingers held
the night before to the candle and pulled back?
Did the loud prayer cried into the brutal

wind for mercy on his judges distract his ears
from the sizzling of his sweat drops in the fire?
I remember how, as children, we fed each other's morbid
fascination: "If you could choose, how would you die?"

We never allowed the peaceful midnight passing,
the gentle slumbering final breath, but listed
awful choices: hanging, beheading, drowning, falling
from great heights, lingering sickness, bullets to the heart.

Burning was the worst. And so the martyrs burned
at the stake stopped me, stop me still, to try to fathom
unfathomable faith and call to mind
another childhood ritual tempting the finite

mind to defy its finitude: "How much do you love me?"
And always the only answer that served mocked
the question even as it reassured, with arms spread wide
but never wide enough: "This much."

—Marilyn Chandler McEntyre

Deluge

130

Friend,
our easy play
is naked silent desire.
You quiver
at the calm curve
of Heaven's fountain.
Yes, sing, Zenith,
live talk ache fight
scream,
For Majestic Time
has dark grace,
will excite
show bare sorrow
ring hell
tear out true fire.

—Josephine Carson

FIRE

Phantom Life

A year of trouble is a gate in the mind,
here you are with new shoes
outside in the rain, you can't recall
what page you were on,
but you'd swear it was good.

Books dim on their shelves,
they hang around the walls of your room,
aching away like a phantom life.
You can read what you used to think
any time you can bear to look,
the way the barb wire scar you got at five
is still there, pale moon to remind you.

Voices of the past rise up like a stammer,
like the voices who lived on
in the burned house next door. Come back,
they cry out. Undo, remember.
Your story, however, is slipping away.

University, hospital, lover, let them all
learn to take care of themselves.

—Karen Fiser

Confessions

—for my older sister

It is too soon to tell you this—
that thirty years ago
I watched you undress from the dark
of the hallway,
through your door that never latched,
through my shame, my rooting curiosity,
that yours were the first breasts
to drive me to Father Walsh's confessional,
ten Hail Marys
and ten Acts of Contrition
the easy price of his forgiveness.

In the recovery room you've awakened
again as the flat-chested girl
I never knew you as,
the one whose inscrutable ripening
would make you the object
of neighborhood jokes,
of names you could have died from.
This morphined afternoon,
I would unswaddle you,
wrap your centipede scars
in fresh white cotton,
a gauzy summer dress
to keep this slow penance
from becoming your life.

—Arthur Nahill

"By Fidelity is Grace Sustained"

Lie down on the grass and listen to the birds,
Steep yourself in delicious idleness . . .
By fidelity in little things is grace sustained,
Pure sand of the sea and variegated shells,

Tall floods and silver veils, their secret source
Somewhere beneath the soft grass where we threw
Ourselves most lovingly, where sparkling salamanders
Floated amidst the broken light, the flames

Rippling without our aid or intervention,
Lovingly as if your dew-soaked soles
Were to be wiped quite clean, and dried again
By the astonished sunlight or my hand

Lifted while I half-weeping and half-smiling
Ask if you'll ever leave . . . Now bear me over
To that gliding isle that lies before us
So full of strange anxieties and dreams

That even the tufts of sedge seem possessed of a soul
I would not call my own by artifice,
Design, or compromise. The power to love
And suffer is but one power, and it's yours

As well, should you choose to take it. Take it now
Before you decide to cast me off, before
The flames rise or the broken light is mended,
Wiped clean by the sunlight or my hand.

—Ned Balbo

Jinn

The wind broke into my house, broke open
storm doors at night, and cracked the walls I've leant upon

Hoarse is the voice, the new and the old in song together,
Bring the flourish of fertile months under your skin to the surface.
Leave open the house. We know and in your dreams have lightly
stepped,
        the painful fractures shown.
These are yours to mind with us. Keep an eye open in.
Be in the treble at the back of your head, and the bass in your spine.
        We, the flute, will come a note or two.
We hold the harbinger tongues and speak with flame to burn away
        the half of who you claim will hold you back.

—Mandy Richmond Dowd

On Watching "Remembrance of the Camps (1945)"

establish
voice over
zoom

how ornate the
iron gate

how little muscle
walks
how many bones

how wide
the starving
smile

how the bunk turtle
cranes
unblinking
at the camera

how dragging chins
streak
the dirt

how strong the ones
who push the cart

how ecumenical
the feeding
of 5000
to trench No. 8

how the socket
stares

how the penis
lasts

how white the yarmulke
of snow
on skull

how urgent
the reach
frozen
in fire

how the typhoid flea
rides out
the flame

how expressionistic
the char

how neatly made
the barbed wire
bed

how by the millions
striped pants and tunics
are saved

how long the line
of citizens
to see the skinbox
the pelvis paperweight
the framed tattoo

how the tiny black head
of the Polish engineer
sneers
on its trivet

how joy is left
to children

how the fed
inherit all

how the wind
drowns a voice

how many blades
rise
through a plowed field

credits

—Randall VanderMey

Rebuilding Jerusalem

Your ancient ruins shall be rebuilt (Isaiah 58:12)

Rejoice with Jerusalem in joy, all you who mourn over her,
that you may suck and be satisfied with her consoling breasts;
that you may drink deeply with delight from the abundance of her glory. . . .
You shall be carried upon her hip, and dandled upon her knees, and you
shall be comforted in Jerusalem. (Isaiah 66:13)

It had been a city of turrets and towers,
A lone tomb now, a ruin,
The vast arches cracked, the rooms—
Where shuttles had purred and pages turned,
Where strings had vibrated in the tangy twilight—
Crumbled.
Stories had been told here, and here herbs bred for healing.

The wreck wasted in the sharp shadow
Of a mountain whose snow filaments
Streaked the absorbent earth.

Stumbling on the rubble
A traveler one morning
Floundered through stones
And ripped pavement
Wondering about its story.

Charred bones of wood where a beam had burned,
Heaped in a mass grave. A wind stirred,
Grey ashes fluttered.

Two sundered walls, no longer ceilinged,
Had succumbed to the beating
(Of fire? of water?)
A third, almost fallen,
Retained yet a corner,
Two stones vertical.

In that angle a fledgling pigeon,
White feathers ash-lined,
Nestled in the wreck.
And this soft warbler, tinged but not tainted,

FIRE

Braided a song for the weighed-down wanderer,
A thread in the unraveled ruin.

One woven rope, one unbroken cord
For the hand of a climber to hold
On the ledge, on the edge of a fall,
On the lip of a cliff:
A call, a connection, a hope.

The traveler touched the swaying rope,
With wrist and skull he circled the skein,
Hauled himself up the snow-veined height,
Invisibly steadied on borders of blue stones.
The coarse strand, feeling of feathers stroked backward,
Softened to silk as the fibers spiraled
Aligning themselves like a woman's belt.

Knowing by crawling
He scaled the mountain,
Felt stone turn tender
Under his hand.
The rock was living, the mountain moved.
A woman's arm offered
To cradle the climber
In the swell of a valley,
The lap of her skirt.

Clutching his swinging safety
He craned to see
If walls could breathe,
If granite grows lungs.
The nod of the woman released
His hand, which reached to suckle.

In that nursing the City murmured
And he filled his mouth with milk,
Brimming in cream, in milk,
Till ready to dream
He rested on the wrinkled ranks of cloth
And curled into a question mark of thanks.

—Wendy-Marie Teichert

"Why not be wholly changed into fire?"
—Abbot Lot, 4th Century

138

After the breathtaking volta,
after what must have happened
in the white space,

I came back to find you gone.
Then dreamed the dream that I was made
of words, not flesh and bone.

But if the body were a kind of book,
with veins of ink, a spine all red and gold,
could we dance and turn

under the maple's inferno of color,
color spilled like wine across the skin,
color seen so clearly it is pain,

infinite yet temporal,
like music, as if the great tree's color
were its only way to sing.

—Karen Fiser

FIRE

In midday sun
the old man sits in the rose garden
still as other roses

On my nightly walk
at the schoolyard
the bright moon appears

Three lights this evening:
the moon, the candle,
and my son reading haiku

—John McEntyre

CONTRIBUTORS

Norma Almquist
Los Angeles, California

Erik Anderson-Reece
Lexington, Kentucky

Ila R. Asplund
Seattle, Washington

Ned Balbo
Baltimore, Maryland

Allison Benis
Irvine, California

Josephine Carson
San Francisco, California

Robert Chianese
Ventura, California

Kevin Clark
San Luis Obispo, California

Steve Cook
Santa Barbara, California

Mark DeCarteret
Portsmouth, New Hampshire

Lahna Diskin
Yardley, Pennsylvania

Mandy Richmond Dowd
Oakland, California

John Drexel
Glen Ridge, New Jersey

Karen Fiser
Charlottesville, Virginia

Jane Fremon
West Trenton, New Jersey

Martin Galvin
Chevy Chase, Maryland

Mark Gibbons
Pablo, Montana

Molly Giles
San Francisco, California

Roger Hecht
Syracuse, New York

Edwin Honig
Warwick, Rhode Island

Andrejika Beth Hough
New York, New York

Meg Kearney
New York, New York

Ron Lawrence
Los Angeles, California

Colleen Lindsay
San Francisco, California

Stephen Massimilla
Sea Cliff, New York

John McEntyre
Santa Barbara, California

Marilyn Chandler McEntyre
Santa Barbara, California

Carla Mengel
Santa Barbara, California

Arthur Nahill
Arlington, Massachusetts

Jeanne Nichols
Los Angeles, California

Linden F. Ontjes
Los Angeles, California

Sharon Page
Oakland, California

Charlotte Painter
San Francisco, California

Robert Parham
Florence, South Carolina

Ben Passikoff
Flushing, New York

Louis Phillips
New York, New York

Rhonda C. Poynter
Berkeley, California

C.A. Prettiman
Emmaus, Pennsylvania

Mediha Saliba
Tarzana, California

David Starkey
Aurora, Illinois

Annie Stenzel
El Cerrito, California

Marc Swan
Centerville, Massachusetts

Craig Taylor
Rohnert Park, California

Mary Teichert
Boston, Massachusetts

Wendy-Marie Teichert
Sacramento, California

Gustavo Alberto Garcia Vaca
Los Angeles, California

Paul Willis
Santa Barbara, California

Cindy LaFavre Yorks
Villa Park, California

Randy VanderMey
Santa Barbara, California